SENSEI TENNIS

SENSEI TENNIS

Martial Arts *(and More!)* in the MASTERY OF TENNIS

MARK A. BEEDE AND JOHN NELSON

Copyright © 2018 by Mark A. Beede and John Nelson.

Library of Congress Control Number:		2018908560
ISBN:	Hardcover	978-1-9845-4191-8
	Softcover	978-1-9845-4190-1
	eBook	978-1-9845-4189-5

All rights reserved. No part of this book may be reproduced or transmitted in any form or by any means, electronic or mechanical, including photocopying, recording, or by any information storage and retrieval system, without permission in writing from the copyright owner.

The views expressed in this work are solely those of the author and do not necessarily reflect the views of the publisher, and the publisher hereby disclaims any responsibility for them.

Any people depicted in stock imagery provided by Getty Images are models, and such images are being used for illustrative purposes only. Certain stock imagery © Getty Images.

Print information available on the last page.

Rev. date: 07/30/2018

To order additional copies of this book, contact:
Xlibris
1-888-795-4274
www.Xlibris.com
Orders@Xlibris.com
775194

Sensei TENNIS

MARK A. BEEDE AND JOHN NELSON

CONTENTS

FOREWORD By Dick Gould, Emeritus: Men's Tennis Coach and Director of Tennis, Stanford University ix

PREFACE xi

INTRODUCTION Tennis, Martial Arts, And The Fundamentals Of Athletic Performance xiii

Chapter 1	Growth And Learning Mind-Set 1
Chapter 2	Discipline And Purposeful Practice 6
Chapter 3	Attitude, Confidence, Fearlessness, And Pressure 11
Chapter 4	Concentration And Staying In The Present 31
Chapter 5	Calmness And Relaxation 36
Chapter 6	Ying And Yang: Flow And Force 38
Chapter 7	Breathing 41
Chapter 8	Connectedness And Visualization The Mind And Body As One 43
Chapter 9	Simplicity 60
Chapter 10	Anticipation, Perception, And Reaction 61
Chapter 11	Movement, Setup, And Balance 75
Chapter 12	Ground Force And The Kinetic Chain 87
Chapter 13	Putting It All Together: Rotation And Striking 96
Chapter 14	Strategy And Tactics 104
Chapter 15	General Principles Of Stroking In Tennis 117
Chapter 16	The Forehand 134
Chapter 17	The Backhand 145
Chapter 18	The Volley, Overhead, And Drop Shot 155
Chapter 19	The Serve 163
Chapter 20	The Return 173
Chapter 21	Doubles 179

Chapter 22	Drills	182
Chapter 23	Physical Fitness And Training	194

CONCLUSION 199
ACKNOWLEDGMENTS 201
REFERENCES 205
ABOUT THE AUTHORS 209
INDEX 213

FOREWORD

JOHN NELSON—a name that stands out in collegiate tennis at the highest echelon! Few, if any, could have accomplished what John has done as a program builder and at schools with substantially less than the NCAA allowable support—from Cal State Hayward to UC Davis to San Diego State and in Hawaii. He has had five Mountain West Championships and a Sweet 16 Division I finish, and he is a coach whose top players have successfully competed with the best players in the country—a man whose high principles and ethics should be a lesson to us all.

When I think of excellence, achievement against incredible odds, one who does things the "right way," and one who gets the absolute most out of his players and teams, I think immediately of John Nelson! His quiet demeanor belies his fierce competitiveness. He has truly earned and merited the admiration and respect of his players and his peers.

I have had the great pleasure of knowing John for many, many years. I have watched him grow and mature into a "player's coach" and a "coach's coach." He has always represented his players, program, university, and our coaching profession in the highest manner. Many of my best players have ended up on the wrong side of the net from a Nelson-coached opponent!

So you can imagine how honored I was to be asked by John and coauthor Mark Beede to write a foreword to their book, and I immediately accepted because of my great faith and belief in John. Then I learned of their title, *Sensei Tennis*, introducing the fundamentals of tennis, which John knows and coaches so well, *only* after a presentation of the "Fundamentals of Athletic Performance," as illustrated in the understanding the martial arts! This is completely new to me, and I must admit I hesitated on my commitment to John. But as I read on, I slowly bought into the martial arts credo that "the mind is one's best weapon," that maximum performance is absolutely intertwined with the spiritual, mental, and emotional, as well as the physical.

The martial arts principles of a growth and learning mind-set, discipline, attitude, staying in the present, calmness, breathing, simplicity, an understanding of force, rotation and strategy, balance and movement, to name a few, relate to so much more in life than simply striking a tennis ball. John Nelson and Mark Beede's *Sensei Tennis* is just a great balance of East and West. As I did, give John and Mark's book a chance. You will be glad you did, and you will be not only a better athlete and tennis player but also a better person because of it. Finally, I have figured out some extra reasons for John's success . . .

Dick Gould
Emeritus: Men's Tennis Coach, Director of Tennis
Stanford University

PREFACE

Why pick up and read a book on tennis when the first chapter about stroking a tennis ball doesn't occur until later, much later?

Why? Because the basic components of athletic performance, tennis included, involve fundamentals even more basic and inherent than physical technique. The basic fundamentals of athletic performance must first come from within.

In this book we strive to explain the fundamentals of tennis, and athletic performance generally, through the time-honored principles of martial arts. One can master technique but will fall short of athletic mastery without first mastering himself, without developing a state of being that martial arts' ancient precepts acknowledge as necessary.

If you desire to improve your game through learning forehands, backhands, serves, returns, volleys, and other tennis shots, this book is for you. But first, focus on the inner you. The fundamentals of athletic performance involve much, much more than mere physical mastery; the true fundamentals of athletic performance involve personal mastery.

Hence, a book about tennis and athletic performance that focuses first on personal mastery, on the inner fundamentals that allow one to maximize external performance by improving the inner self. If you want to become a better person while improving your tennis game, this book is for you.

Time-honored principles of martial arts acknowledge the need for a strong, serene, relaxed, and focused inner psychic core before physical mastery can occur. *Sensei Tennis* provides that focus for tennis by using the fundamentals of martial arts.

We hope that you will choose to read this book not only to learn more about tennis and about how to perform better in sport but also to learn more about yourself and improve as a person.

Take each chapter and consider its significance. Many may tend to pass off some fundamentals as superfluous, but they are not. Each chapter involves a true fundamental, a necessary building block for the master athlete. Work to master each chapter and incorporate each lesson into your personal psyche and physical performance so that you can become the best you can be. That's why you should pick up and read this book.

INTRODUCTION

TENNIS, MARTIAL ARTS, AND THE FUNDAMENTALS OF ATHLETIC PERFORMANCE

Tradition and history place martial arts as one of the oldest forms of competition and sport, spanning a course of thousands of years. Tennis, thought of by many as a sport rich in tradition, compared to martial arts is a baby in swaddling clothes. While martial arts has over two thousand years' experience, Wimbledon, the world's most tradition-based and revered tennis championship, is less than 150 years old! Tennis and other sports have much to learn from evolved and established martial arts principles, including biomechanics, psychology, and ethics.

Revered, respected, and honored, the principles of martial arts are time-tested, true, and biomechanically correct. With thousands of years of tradition and experience, the test of time has culled the weak and the wrong. Like wheat from the chaff, the test of time has winnowed the right from the wrong. Developed through self-defense and war, the incorrect sensei's wrong martial arts methods and techniques died, often in battle, with him and his followers, leaving to survive the right and the true.

Developing and emanating from the East (Asia), martial arts carries a mystical, almost magical allure, an exotic sense, particularly for those from the West who are brought up on the so-called traditional sports of baseball, basketball, tennis, golf, and football. For the uninitiated, the ability of masters to perform seemingly magical acts of breaking concrete blocks and slabs of wood with bare hands and feet is unbelievable, even when directly observed. Many think that there is some magical, transcendental trick to performing these acts, when in fact it is all about the right attitude, concentration, and the natural laws of physics.

Marrying martial arts and Eastern philosophy, one looks to Asian principles of *natural law*, the force that rules everyone's body and mind. When referring to the body and physical forces, this Asian natural law is physics, pure and simple.

We all, as reasonably intelligent people, trust physics throughout our normal lives. For instance, when flying in an airplane, we trust our lives to the physics of aerodynamics. When in a tall building, we naturally trust our lives to the physics of structural engineering. So what happens when we, as reasonably intelligent people, play tennis, a mere game? *We ignore physics!* Let's instead use the common sense and trust we use in our lives throughout each day to play a mere game. Trust in physics to improve and perform better.

While one, remembering one's first Westernized physics class, will picture Newton under the apple tree and a vague memory of formulas quantifying the forces of nature and physics, the traditional Asian martial arts perspective provides a different view *of the same forces*. From the traditional Asian martial arts view, rather than talking about angular or linear momentum, one refers to ying, yang, and ki.

No matter which martial art you study, the same fundamentals exist. Whether you are in Japan studying judo, aikido, karate, or jujitsu; in China practicing tai chi, kung fu, or wing chun; in Korea learning taekwondo; or in the Philippines taking on arnis and kali, the same fundamentals apply. We call these the lowest common denominators. In fact, these are the lowest common denominators for almost all sports, for almost all physical activity, and for almost all performance. Whether this is open to argument as applying to all sports, the lowest common denominator fundamentals common to all martial arts definitely apply to tennis.

So what are these fundamentals? The typical and traditional Western athlete and coach first looks to the physical, with secondary regard and sometimes willful ignorance of the nonphysical "intangibles." Not so with martial arts. Martial arts fundamentals include and involve all aspects of being: the spiritual, mental, emotional, and of course the physical.

Your mind is your best weapon. Most athletes and coaches start by emphasizing and accentuating the physical and then, perhaps on a rainy day, if at all, supplement physical training with psychological, mental, and emotional readiness. Particularly in the West, many see the spiritual, mental, and emotional foci and emphases as relatively irrelevant concerns to day-to-day training. Whether they admit it or not, many mistakenly consider these aspects as inherently fixed in the person, not subject to development or change. Consequently, they miss out on vital areas of development and performance. Martial arts dramatically bear out the mind's importance. Thousands of years of development show that the spirit, mind, and emotions are as essential to develop as the body and physical techniques.

Therefore, the following fundamentals differ from what some may expect. Many of the Western old-school coaches in other purported mainstream sports minimize the so-called intangibles, suggesting that much is meaningless soft psychobabble. They do so at their peril and to their players' detriment. The fundamentals of martial arts and, for that matter, athletic achievement involve much, much more than mere physical mastery. In fact, the intangibles are fundamental to mastery, just as fundamental as the physical. Without mastering *each* fundamental, whether intangible or physical, the athlete will fail to master his craft, whether in martial arts or otherwise.

FUNDAMENTALS

1. Growth and Learning Mind-Set
2. Discipline and Purposeful Practice
3. Attitude, Confidence, and Fearlessness
4. Concentration and Staying in the Present
5. Calmness and Relaxation
6. Ying and Yang: Flow and Force
7. Breathing
8. Connectedness: The Mind and Body as One
9. Simplicity
10. Anticipation, Perception, and Reaction: Readiness for the Greatest Threat
11. Movement, Balance, and Setup
12. Ground Force and the Kinetic Chain
    - Legs and Hips
    - Core
    - Upper Torso and Shoulders
    - Head
    - Arms and Hands
13. Rotation and Striking
    - Angular Momentum
    - Strike through the Target
14. Strategy and Tactics
    - Take Your Opponent Off-Balance
    - Distraction
    - Don't Fight Force with Force: Go with the Flow
    - Vary Your Attack

These fundamentals, or lowest common denominators, include the mental and emotional as well as the physical. Frankly, once you condition and tune your body to master techniques and tactics, it is the mental and emotional that make the difference. The challenges with Westernized-style training are that techniques and tactics are developed often to the *exclusion* of the mental and emotional. To perform optimally, the athlete needs to develop everything. Furthermore, it is never too early to work on anything.

The lowest common denominators demonstrate the integral components to sport. By focusing on these basic athletic principles, you become a true athlete. Transcending individual sport, these principles show how the athlete and his body can perform efficiently and effectively throughout the realm of sport, work, and physical activity.

So what are we talking about when we look at martial arts and then apply those principles to tennis and other sports? We're talking about many things, including attitude, physical fitness, mental fitness, and biomechanics. The first portion of any training program must deal with the individual's attitude and awareness, what his goals are, and what he wants to achieve from any program or sport. Of course physical fitness, including strength, endurance, and flexibility, is also important. The combination of physical and mental fitness is essential to achieve maximum potential.

In studying the basic principles of sports and athletics, it is interesting to note that many of the basic fundamentals, physical and mental, overlap from one fundamental and one sport to another. For example, consider baseball. While martial arts evolved as systems of self-defense and survival, baseball evolved as America's pastime. Like tennis, baseball is a game, a game of big business in America, attracting many of North, Central, and South America's finest athletes.

Tim Robson's baseball book *The Hitting Edge: How to Excel at the Plate* is remarkable in the knowledge and expertise laid out. While focusing on how to hit a baseball, it is amazing how many of the principles Robson examines apply directly to tennis and other sports. Robson, a professional coach who has spent his life studying, playing, and practicing his craft as a player and coach, clearly knows what he is talking about. The marriage of theory, the need for practice, mental and emotional clarity, balance, and kinetic chain all apply to baseball and tennis, just as with martial arts. We believe that almost all sports require mastery of similar principles for excellence and success.

Body position biomechanics remain the same throughout sport, whether one is into martial arts, baseball, basketball, golf, tennis, or dancing for that matter. Keep your balance. Keep your elbows in front. Keep your head still. Be ready to move forward.

In martial arts, tennis, and other sports, the most important factors are balance and movement. To achieve greatness, one must also master attitude and technique.

The Western style of focusing on specific techniques with results carries some advantages, but all too often, those advantages are constrained by a failure to utilize what the East has to offer. Combine the East with the West. Study and practice to merge the West's benefits with the East's advantages. Accept the East, study the East, practice the East, and you can unleash amazing energy, flow, strength, and power in whatever you do, including tennis. However, acceptance involves more than just an open mind and intellectual belief; you must practice, and then you must practice more.

CHAPTER ONE

GROWTH AND LEARNING MIND-SET

Those of us raised in a traditional Western culture have been brought up focusing on results, on winning and not losing, on succeeding and not failing. Whatever others might say, results are key; results are the end-all. Unfortunately, while we all recognize that a game looks toward a result and establishing a winner, the Western outlook has some counterproductive tendencies. Focusing on results places in many not only a drive to achieve but also a drive to not fail, which naturally instills fear.

Process and growth are the Eastern way as opposed to the result-driven Western way. Dr. Carol Dweck's seminal psychological work *Mindset: The New Psychology of Success* criticizes the traditional Western result-oriented approach to education in specific and life in general.

In the West, we are taught to get high grades. Learning, if it happens, happens as a result of achieving the A grade. Learning is secondary; the proverbial holy grail is the straight A report card. Dweck disagrees with this approach, even accusing it as counterproductive. She sees this as producing a fixed mind-set, a mind-set that fights learning, growth, and development. With a fixed mind-set, people worry about the straight As, worry about being number one, worry about what others think, and worry about where they stand right now in relation to others. Dweck sees this as stultifying and static, as fixed . . . and not good.

Instead, Dweck convincingly teaches that the real road to learning is a journey and process, the embracing of a growth mind-set. To truly *learn*, one must embrace the actual *learning*, not the result, enjoying the path and the way. We agree. To truly *perform*, embrace the actual *performing*, not the result; enjoy the process. To truly *compete*, embrace the actual *competing*; let the result be the secondary end. Enjoy the process. Enjoy the journey while growing and developing along the way.

Paradoxically, by embracing the journey, by actually focusing on *learning, performing, and competing* rather than winning and losing, one actually *increases* the chances of winning. By not focusing on winning, one wins more.

Returning for a moment to the fixed mind-set ideal type, the fixed mind-set mentality and culture impose expectations. Sometimes those expectations pressure an individual to achieve, perhaps even beyond his abilities; sometimes those expectations impose boundaries well below an individual's potential.

Let us give an example from coauthor John Nelson's experience. John grew up with an identical twin brother, Jeff. Throughout their youth, John and Jeff were practically inseparable in almost everything they did. They played together, competed together, were in the same classes together, and studied together—they did everything together.

At one time, concerns arose that brothers Jeff and John were spending too much time together that perhaps they should separate in some fashion purportedly to develop more separate identities. Consequently, Jeff and John, who previously took most of their classes together, were split into separate math classes, with Jeff staying in the advanced math class and John moving from the higher-to a lower-achieving class.

Previously, both Jeff and John were learning and doing well in math, producing similar good results and grades. However, with the separation, while Jeff continued to learn and perform in the higher group, John's performance lagged and deteriorated.

Why? John attributes his decline to lower expectations. While his brother continued to learn and progress in an environment pushing for higher achievement, John's new setting had lower expectations, and John adapted accordingly. He adjusted his learning to lowered expectations, and his performance declined.

While in other areas, Jeff and John remained together, and their achievement levels remained on similar tracks, their respective math performances diverged significantly. While Jeff continued to learn and achieve, comparatively John did not.

Then, John and Jeff were placed back together in the same math class. Lo and behold! John's results improved! John looks at these events as an indication that limiting expectations limits achievement and performance.

The message: Do not limit your expectations! Do not get caught in a fixed mind-set. Do not allow others to limit you. Keep an open, receptive mind.

In *Striking Thoughts: Bruce Lee's Wisdom for Daily Living*, the iconic martial artist recounts the story of the empty tea cup.

> *A learned man once went to visit a Zen teacher to inquire about Zen. As the Zen teacher talked, the learned man frequently interrupted to express his own opinion about this or that.*
>
> *Finally, the Zen teacher stopped talking and began to serve tea to the learned man. He poured the cup full, then kept pouring until the cup overflowed.*
>
> *"Stop!" said the learned man. "The cup is full, no more can be poured in."*

> *"Like this cup, you are full of your own opinions,"* replied the Zen teacher. *"If you do not first empty your cup, how can you taste my cup of tea?"*[1]

Welcome the test of learning. Learn from everyone and everything: your sensei, your opponents, your training partners, your practices, your wins, and your losses. With learning and growth in mind, everyone works with you, not against you. Empty your cup and keep an open mind.

Everyone makes mistakes; learn through your mistakes. Face and do new things. Be not afraid to fail; see failure as an opportunity for growth.

When training in the dojo or on the tennis court, grow and learn by cooperating with those around you. Adopt the "dojo environment," keeping a conducive learning atmosphere. Your "opponents" while training are your partners. In a genuine dojo atmosphere, everyone works and trains by learning from each other. Work with your partner, help him with his techniques and weakness, and in a good dojo, he will help you with yours. Through this growth-centered and cooperative process, everyone, including you, improves.

Robson seems to also recognize this in his book, noting that being positive and allowing hitters to make mistakes without fear of failure as they learn motivate most hitters to reach their top potential. Motivation to succeed must come from within; coaches can only facilitate and help it along.

---

[1] Golf teaching professional Bob Vocker says that there are two professionals at every golf lesson, the actual professional and the one in the student's head. If the one in the head thinks he knows more than the actual pro, the student will never learn or even hear what the actual pro is saying. Empty the cup.

Golf is no exception to the need for a growth mind-set. In his book *I Feel Your Pain: Let's Make Golf Uncomplicated*, Mike Malaska notes that golf is a journey. The key is to be motivated by successes and failures, and then you will try again tomorrow.

The bottom line is that you are on a journey, and your true competition is yourself, not others. With a growth mind-set, you learn from anyone and everyone and from every situation. A true martial artist, a true athlete, an authentic person travels a journey of growth and learning, applying his calmness and problem-solving abilities not only to his craft but also to life. The growth mind-set applies to everything in life, whether in martial arts, school, relationships, baseball, golf, or tennis.

Remember:
Keep a growth mind-set.
Enjoy the present.
Stay in the moment.
Focus on the process rather than on the result.

CHAPTER TWO

DISCIPLINE AND PURPOSEFUL PRACTICE

The Definition of Discipline

*Do What You Should Do,
Every Time,
To the Best of Your Ability*

You must connect the mental and emotional with the physical. You must develop and maintain confidence, a calm state of mind, and a focused outlook. How to connect all these together? With purposeful practice. With repetitions to the point that reaction and movement become almost instinctual and unthinking, subliminal and implicit. By developing strength, endurance, and flexibility, one develops both body and mind to perform optimally.

Discipline body and mind. It takes discipline to learn each fundamental and to connect everything. It takes discipline to purposefully practice to attain mastery. Through discipline and purposeful practice, do what you should do the best you can do, every time you do. Through this you will improve, perhaps slowly, but surely.

Train slow. Take your time to master your techniques, slowly, repetitively to the point they become automatic, implicit. With disciplined, purposeful repetition, train your techniques so that you can let go, unconsciously performing them, letting them happen. Good techniques flow when mastered.

A common martial arts training technique is to practice *kata*. *Kata* is training specific techniques slowly, very slowly. In performing *kata*, one goes through his motions in super slow motion, isolating each element of each move with steadiness, balance, and precision. Especially when done before a mirror, *kata* provides immediate feedback and helps isolate specific areas requiring improvement.

As *kata* works for martial arts, it also works for tennis. Practice *kata* with your tennis strokes. Go through each stroke in super slow motion while standing in front of a mirror. While performing *kata*, imagine that you are stroking a real ball under real circumstances; isolate each portion of each stroke, and practice repeatedly, over and over. Practice your slow-motion *kata* for each stroke until everything becomes automatic in both slow motion and real time.

One can't hope to perform any new motion at a high level until one masters every subtlety of that motion through practice, practice, and more practice. Ease of movement comes through repetition of the fundamentals. In the dojo, on the baseball field, on the golf course, or on the tennis court, there is simply no other way. *Kata* helps, as do constant repetitions in real time.

The key to mastering new motions, whether in martial arts, golf, or tennis, is to turn new motions into old ones. As Ted Kiegiel notes in *Balanced Golf: Harnessing the Simplicity, Focus, and Natural Motions of Martial Arts to Improve Your All-Around Game*, turning new motions into old allows one to feel the body's power sources, which guide movement. Because the same power sources that rule countless movements in the dojo also rule the golf swing and the tennis stroke, the way to teach martial arts is the perfect approach for zeroing in on proper power source usage for players of any skill level in other sports, including tennis.

A good swing, whether in baseball, golf, or tennis, comes only with practice and sound fundamentals. By accepting martial arts' basic precepts and the philosophy of the East, you unleash your personal potential from the ground up. But you must practice—everything.

It's not easy to practice hard every time. It takes a mentally strong and committed athlete to put in the time needed to excel at the next level. The old saying "Practice makes perfect" should really be "Perfect practice makes perfect."

Discipline your mind. Develop habits of focus and steadiness. Regularly review your thoughts, feelings, and performance. Consider establishing a journal where you write down your daily experiences and feelings. A journal helps maintain focus and proper introspection as to how you are doing, physically and emotionally. While it takes time, valuable time off the court, for many it is time well spent.

Practice purposefully, always. Today, make yourself better than yesterday. Tomorrow, make yourself better than today. Whether practicing or competing, keep your focus on the task. Keep trying to improve. Purposeful practice is the only path to steady and genuine improvement. Don't just put in the time; put in purposeful time and practice with the focused genuine intent to improve; *and do it every day.*

In baseball, Robson notes that success requires year-round training. Good players take the time and effort to keep themselves strong and fit during the off-season or school breaks. Physical conditioning is very important for any athlete. Playing baseball by itself doesn't keep a player physically fit. To excel, one must work extra and work smart. The same rings true for tennis—especially for tennis.

Excellence requires time and sacrifice. As David Foster Wallace notes in *String Theory*, a compilation of brilliant tennis articles, "We prefer not to countenance the kinds of sacrifices the professional-athlete has made to get so good at one particular thing. . . . [T]he realities of top-level athletics today require an early and total commitment to one pursuit. An almost ascetic focus." Later, in discussing former top 100 player Michael Joyce's commitment to tennis and work ethic, Wallace says that "the restrictions on his life have been, in my opinion, grotesque. . . . But the radical compression of his attention and self has allowed him to become a transcendent practitioner of an art—something few of us get to be. It's allowed him to visit and test parts of his psyche that most of us do not even know for sure we have, to manifest in concrete forms virtues like courage, persistence in the face of pain or exhaustion, performance under wilting scrutiny and pressure."

Almost everyone agrees that hard work and more hard work are required, but how much hard work can one expect to expend before reaching his potential and, hopefully, mastering his craft? Matthew Syed's book *Bounce: The Myth of Talent and the Power of Practice* is well worth reading. Full of anecdotes and relying on scientific studies and surveys, *Bounce* underscores and emphasizes the need for hard work and practice.

Examining professions, such as music and firefighting, multiple sports, and games, such as chess, Syed persuasively argues that ten thousand hours of purposeful practice and experience are required for anyone to master his craft, whatever it is.

Think about it. Ten thousand hours is a lot of time. Ten thousand hours involves years and years of purposeful intense work. To achieve mastery in anything, including martial arts, baseball, golf, or tennis, ten thousand hours is required time.

***Remember:**
**Practice makes permanent.
Practice hitting the correct shot
with the correct speed and spin
to a target
each and every time
you stroke the ball.**

CHAPTER THREE

ATTITUDE, CONFIDENCE, FEARLESSNESS, AND PRESSURE

Compete
Compete with attitude.
Compete confidently.
Compete fearlessly.
Enjoy the battle, win or lose.
Welcome pressure.
Embrace pressure.
Compete . . . now.

What is attitude? The Oxford English Dictionary defines *attitude* as "a way of thinking or feeling." Now, to maximize performance, what is the right attitude?

The right attitude comes down to desire. Human emotions mobilize the mind and body. The key with attitude is to achieve the right emotions and the right desires to perform well.

The right attitude is the desire to perform and compete and continually maintain that desire to compete, even in the face of adversity. There is an attitude in fighting: you may hurt me, but I will win. Accept the challenge and embrace the fight. When knocked down, get back up.

Humility is a good thing. Never underestimate anyone. There is always someone who knows more than you and who is better than you. Respect your sensei, respect your opponents, and respect everyone.

Minimize anger. Anger *will* betray you unless you channel and control your emotions.

Remember that attitude is a choice and often a matter of perspective. You can choose to be positive, or you can choose to be negative. Accentuate the positive.

Think of a flying airplane. When the plane is going up, one part of the plane is going up, but in a sense, the plane is also pointing down. It is all a matter of perspective. When one wing tilts up, the other wing tilts down. Really, the plane is the same, but the different perspective puts it in a different light.

Attitude is much like the flying plane. You can take the negative attitude like the wing or tail pointing down, or you can look at things positively as if the nose or wing is pointing up. The better perspective is to keep a positive, upbeat attitude. The choice is yours.

When it comes to attitude, tennis Grand Slam champion Stan Wawrinka's forearm tattoo quotes Irish author Samuel Beckett's *Worstward Ho*:

> *Ever tried.*
> *Ever failed.*
> *No matter.*
> *Try again.*
> *Fail again.*
> *Fail better.*

Perseverance and grit: Learn it. Get it. Use it. Keep it.

Lose the Ego
Get Out of Your Own Way

The consciousness of self is the greatest hindrance to the proper execution of all physical action.
—Bruce Lee

What gets in the way when the pressure is on and one "needs" to perform? The answer: The ego. Expectations, pressure, anxiety, and the so-called "need" to perform come from the inner ego. Paradoxically, what the ego desires and how it feels usually hinder achieving what it wants. As Tim Gallwey notes in *The Inner Game of Tennis*, the cause of most stress is found in the ego's attachment.

Release the ego. Get out of your own way. Detach yourself. Let the shots flow.

Strength often becomes weakness because the ego invests in strength.

The ego perceives threats. Look for solutions, not for threats. Looking for solutions is positive and forward looking. Looking for solutions promotes flow. On the other side, threats produce fear. Fear distracts. Fear takes one out of the present, out of the now.

Fear produces anxiety. Psychosomatically, anxiety produces tension and muscle tightening. Tightening contracts the muscles, impairing power and flow. Lose the ego; look for solutions. Release the fear; find the flow.

Face your fears. Overcome them. Wrap not your self-worth in results; rather, find your self-worth in learning. With too much to lose, fear sets in.

Instill confidence as part of your attitude. Confidence is a way of thinking or feeling, part of a successful attitude. Confidence does not assure perfect performance. One can be confident while still knowing that mistakes may occur.

A confident person accepts that in competition, mistakes and losing occur. However, a confident person knows that when a mistake or a loss happens, he can handle it. He knows that provided he gives it his best, whatever happens will be all right. That's what having a confident attitude is all about, and with that positive outlook, one puts himself in the optimal mental state to master the situation. As the Psychology Solutions website article "Secrets of Confident People" notes, confident people have positive yet realistic expectations, have faith in their own abilities, and are comfortable with uncertainty.

Confidence is not arrogance. "Secrets of Confident People" further explains that truly confident people are largely unaware of the fact they are confident; they just "are." But when a person starts to believe he's better than his abilities, when he thinks he is better than others, then he verges into "arrogance" territory. This ego-driven false confidence leads to taking risks that are beyond one's ability to handle, and sooner or later, one suffers the sort of catastrophic failure that shatters an overinflated confidence.

The more confidence you have, the less you feel threatened. Conversely, the more you feel threatened, the more fear and tension you feel. Tension destroys power. Fear inhibits you physically and mentally. The more tension you feel, the tighter you become, and the less you can perform. So how to get, improve, and increase confidence? Practice purposefully, and practice more until you act instinctively without thought.

In his book *The Koga Method: Police Weaponless Control and Defense Techniques*, Robert Koga asserts, "Your most important attributes when you approach an explosive situation are your own self-confidence and self-control." Whether engaged in self-defense or tennis, self-confidence and a clear head are essential.

As Koga notes, with self-confidence you'll keep your mind relaxed but constantly alert.

We have talked about attitude as a fundamental of martial arts, and our comments apply throughout sport and life. The right attitude is the desire to compete and perform, maintaining the desire to continue performing, even in the face of adversity. Accept and embrace the challenge, confidently without fear.

Secrets of Proper Attitude

1. More athletes fail through faulty attitude than any other way.
2. Attitudes are habits of thinking. You have the power to develop the habit of thinking thoughts that produce a winning attitude.
3. Positive thoughts are the foundation of a winning attitude.
4. Constantly tell yourself that you can do something, and you will. Tell yourself you can't, and your subconscious will make sure you won't.
5. The desires to prepare and to win are integral parts of a winning attitude.
6. You must first control yourself from within before you scale the heights of athletic greatness. Control your emotions. Master yourself.
7. An athlete with the right attitude is a coachable athlete. He accepts criticism positively and constructively. He constantly strives to learn. He avoids criticizing coaches and teammates.
8. In a team, true success depends on teamwork. The winning attitude prioritizes the team ahead of personal agendas.

9. Your creating a winning attitude is your choice; nothing is more important to succeed.

Tennis

We've talked about the right attitude, the desire to perform, and maintaining the desire to continue performing even in the face of adversity. Your attitude will determine the match's outcome, unless you are completely outclassed by your opponent in other areas. Attitude counts for much more than many think; attitude sets the stage for creating and continuing high performance.

Stay determined. Determination breeds concentration. Determination works for you not only on the inside but also on the outside as your opponent sees and senses your attitude. Your opponent senses when you are determined and resolute; your opponent also senses when you are unsure and not confident. While keeping your resolve, never aid your opponent in any way, especially by showing a lack of sureness or confidence.

Lack of confidence on your part only helps your opponent's confidence. Never say anything to aid your opponent's confidence. Never say "I can't," "I won't," etc. Your opponent should feel that nothing bothers you, that nothing can distract you from what you want. Don't focus on distractions; focus only on what helps you achieve your goal. Stay in the *now*.

Realize that the stronger your will to compete and perform, the tougher you are. Grow that attitude within yourself, and not only you but also your opponents will see it. That attitude alone will build on itself to make you an even tougher competitor.

Before going on the court, accept the day's conditions. Don't worry about them; deal with them. Don't worry about whether the weather is windy, hot, or cold or whether you are a little stiff or slightly injured, or whether the courts are fast, slow, bumpy, or cracked; instead, deal with it. Instead of worrying or complaining, concentrate on how to manage the conditions. Better yet, figure how to use them to your advantage. If it's windy, think of how to use the wind. Your opponent has to play in the same conditions; think how to use the conditions to benefit you; think how those same conditions affect your opponent, and play accordingly.

As you play at higher and higher levels, you necessarily will play better and better players. Recognize that you will play good players, players who can hit winners, balls that you cannot return or perhaps even touch. If your opponent hits a winner, he hits a winner. There is no need to panic. There is no need to worry. Good players hit winners. Respect your opponent; respect your opponent's ball.

What you can do is to control that which you can control. Stay balanced. Show that you are in control and that you won't miss. Keep your attitude. Enjoy the battle even when your opponent plays well.

Control what you can control. Sometimes you can't control whether you win or lose, but you can always control how hard you try and how much effort you put into your match. You can always try your best irrespective of how well your opponent plays. Gallwey asserts that this difference is significant. Maximum effort means concentration, determination, and trusting your body to "let it happen." It means maximum physical and mental effort. Gallwey also notes that the difference between worrying about winning and making the greatest effort to win is subtle but significant.

One can't always control whether he wins or loses, but as Gallwey says, one can always control the *effort* put into winning. One can always try the best he can at any given moment. Additionally, just as accepting a growth mind-set of learning increases the chances of winning, so does focusing on trying the hardest to win increases the chances of winning over one who worries about winning. In short, don't worry about winning or losing; just make sure you try the hardest you can, and the results will take care of themselves.

Control what you can control. Trying your hardest does not mean trying to play great; it simply means trying your hardest to control what you can control. In fact, you should *not* try to play great. *Trying* to play great takes you out of your comfort zone to an area beyond your control. Instead, stay within the zone of what you can control. When playing, do what you can do; and do it well. Your regular stuff is good enough; you don't need to play "*great.*"

A discussion of mental toughness is incomplete without addressing how one can stay tough while taking advantage of his opponent's mental weakness.

Displaying your mental and physical control often produces additional effects beyond just executing your shots. Often your opponent sees this control and, as a result, feels pressure. If your opponent knows that you are in control of yourself, he often will take himself out of his comfort zone in trying to push you out of yours. This is an insidious type of pressure that gradually accumulates, resulting in your opponent trying harder and harder and missing more and more.

Sometimes players set up correctly with balance but then throw themselves off-balance by swinging too hard or by trying to hit too early to get the ball back quickly. They rush to win the point, and miss.

If you have to rush your shot, you're probably hitting the wrong shot. Stay composed. Maintain a champion's composure. Hit the shot you know you have, not the shot you think you might have! Don't rush.

Stay positive. We've all seen those players who laboriously berate themselves seemingly after each missed shot, admonishing themselves, "I'm so bad, I suck." While subconsciously this negative self-criticism is intended to force and improve performance, it usually doesn't work. Chastising oneself actually distracts from the present by providing judgment for the past deed or deeds; once one strays from the present, performance suffers.

Know why you're on the court. Know why you are playing. Know why you are motivated to train and compete. Before you go on the court, know the one reason why you compete, because often, when you go on the court, you'll find a hundred reasons to fail. By keeping your core purpose in mind, you'll keep your will strong.

To see the impact of knowing your "why," view the motivational YouTube video about boxer Buster Douglas's upset knockout of the legendary Mike Tyson at https://www.youtube.com/watch?v=HFcgCrdz-CQ. Challenger Buster Douglas was a heavy underdog and was essentially knocked out by the seemingly invincible Tyson, only to be saved by the bell and then recover to knock out the champion. What was Buster Douglas's "why"? The recent death of his mother.

When you go on the court, what is your "why"? Know what you want; focus on what you want and how to achieve it, and then work to achieve it.

When you miss, don't let it bother you. Move to the next task. Stay positive; you want no emotional downswings on errors.

Rather than judge whether your performance or you have been good or bad, focus on solutions. Believe it or not, you have a choice. You may choose to focus on the negative. You may choose to focus on the positive. Choose the positive; focus on solutions. Focus on doing the right thing *now*.

Between points, take your time. Take the time to make sure that you feel in control, that you are dictating the match's terms.

Let time come to you. There is no need to rush, force your game, or try to do things you cannot do. Play within your limits without trying to force beyond your limits. Know what you can do, and do it.

Always encourage yourself. Don't talk yourself down or get negative. Realize that tennis is not a game of perfection; recognize that you will make errors, so don't let mistakes bother you. If a stroke is off, don't work on it during the match. Make the best of what you can do that day, and do it. Stay positive, and make the best of what you have.

If you get a bad call from your opponent, stand up for your rights. If you're not sure, don't say anything. If it keeps happening, don't confront your opponent; don't get emotional. Simply ask for an umpire and keep your mind at peace. Realize that some players make bad calls intentionally to bother and upset you; others might accuse you of cheating to rattle you. Never get personally involved with your opponent. Maintain your will to compete; nothing can interfere with what you want if you don't let it.

Respect your opponent—always. He may not be as good a player as you, but he is still a person. If you can beat your opponent 6–0, 6–0, do it. Playing an undermatched opponent can still provide good practice as you can still focus, trying to win each point as it happens. However, *never* toy with your opponent no matter how much better you are. You only demean yourself while disrespecting your opponent. Never humiliate your opponent, but beat him as badly as you can. Your opponent will get more out of a 6–0, 6–0 match because he will see how much he needs to improve.

At the end of each match, look your opponent in the eye as you shake hands. Always respect your opponent. Always respect the sport.

At the end of each match, you should feel that you've put out 100 percent effort. Remember that while you cannot always play at the top of your game, you can always try hard.

There are lots of trials and tribulations, lots of "deal with it" moments. Learn to deal with the unexpected things that come up in whatever form they may take, whether it is the weather, opponents, broken equipment, delayed travel, relationships, and so forth. Learn to deal with it.

Pressure goes both ways. It affects you and affects your opponent. How you each handle pressure often dictates who wins.

Pressure is self-made and self-imposed. Often pressure and anxiety come from a disconnect or contradiction between expectations and reality, or the threat of a different reality from what one expects or wants. For instance, living up to others' expectations, living up to a ranking, or expecting a certain result creates pressure. Pressure comes from living outside the present, and it inhibits one from fully living in the moment. Pressure and anxiety usually come from stressing about the result.

Clearly we admonish you to minimize pressure, eliminate your fear, and perform in the present. Despite this, the fact remains that everyone feels pressure. When you feel pressure, don't stress; don't let it impair you. Pressure is often fear; when feeling pressure, embrace your fear. Learn to love the moment. Learn to embrace pressure. Enjoy the challenge. Enjoy the fight.

In his humorously entertaining book *A Handful of Summers* about life on the tour in the '50s and '60s, Gordon Forbes talked about his tennis play and Grand Slam champion and number 1 in the world Rod Laver's play. Let there be no misunderstanding. Gordon Forbes, although self-deprecating in his book, played at a very high level for his time, reaching the top 20 *in the world* and even beating Laver in singles the year Laver won the Grand Slam.

Still, Forbes described his feelings and emotions in competing by saying that "in every close match ever played, you always fought two things—your opponent and the fear inside you, and the worse of the two was the fear." In contrast, Forbes almost deified Laver as having the "ultimate characteristics of the truly great—the ability to become stronger as the competitions tightens. *To play day after day with no fear at all, no sign of strain, but only the positive will to win*" (emphasis added).

Don't worry about what others think. Don't worry about rankings. Don't worry about results. Don't worry about living up to your old self-image. Don't worry. Instead, just do what you can do *now*.

Tennis is not a game of perfection, no matter what we want to think.

Because no one is perfect, including you, worry less about the result than the process. Don't put pressure on yourself to win; instead, put pressure on yourself to play well. In other words, give yourself permission to miss; however, do not give yourself permission to not set up. Not personally permitting mistakes almost necessarily puts you in a position of fear and anxiety. Do not play from fear or from results; instead, play from setting up and hitting targets. Live fully in the moment, and pressure will diminish.

At the same time, while you want to diminish the pressure on you, you also want to increase pressure on your opponent. Pressure accumulates. Often the pressure that breaks an opponent's will is not immediate; rather, it builds up slowly, like a pressure cooker, until the bursting point.

The same principle applies to tennis. Maybe your opponent has a forehand that sometimes breaks down, or perhaps your return is so consistent that your opponent cannot hold serve as easily as he would like. Perhaps you run so hard and cover the court so well that you retrieve and return every ball so that your opponent can't hit the winners he is used to. Perhaps you mix up your pace, shot selection, and placement so that your opponent does not get into a comfortable rhythm and does not have the shots he is most comfortable with. All these scenarios create gradual pressure and discomfort with your opponents. While a single instance may not break your opponent, continually and gradually applying the pressure may well accumulate to the point that he gets so frustrated he loses his will to compete.

Pressure is cumulative; it can break the will. Most do not embrace or like to deal with pressure, so learn to put pressure on your opponent. Know what your opponent is comfortable with and what shot is less comfortable. Pressure is easier to handle at the beginning of a match than at the end. Make your opponent hit big shots under pressure. Eventually, pressure will take its toll.

Early on observe what your opponent's favorite targets are on serves, ground strokes, volleys, and passing shots. Observe your opponent's favorite stroking patterns. Keeping those in mind, know that it's human nature to do what's comfortable under pressure. No one likes pressure, and everyone feels pressure. Does your opponent like to spin the serve to the backhand? Does he like to pass down the line or crosscourt? On a deep approach, does he lob or pass down the line? Know his favorite shots and be ready for those shots when the pressure gets on.

Learn to intimidate. For instance, early in the match, try running around your opponent's second serve to drive a forehand. Let your opponent know you like hitting the forehand so that later, when making the move, you may draw a double fault. Or perhaps you can move in on the second serve, or even chip and charge.

Many sports, including tennis, often come down to a battle of wills. At some point when breaking someone's will, do not let up! Keep coming at him. Every time your opponent hits a weak shot, move in and pressure him. Eventually, your opponent will feel that he always has to hit a good shot against you. *Always hang tough; do not relent!* Sometimes, just by scrapping and getting one more ball back, you can pressure your opponent to the breaking point. You may not always know what makes it happen or when it will occur, but keep the pressure on, and you'll be surprised at what happens.

Many think that there is some sort of magic psychological potion that one can take to become mentally tough and effectively handle pressure. We have given some suggestions through working to play in the present, in the now. There is, also, another valuable technique to help prevent or at least minimize pressure. Is it a magic elixir? No. Is it a quick fix? Definitely not. What is it? The answer: Practice.

Often pressure comes from a lack of confidence and fear, of being unsure about oneself, about what one can do. Practice, practice, and more practice help to make motions and strokes natural, natural to the point that they are subliminally internalized. Super Bowl champion coach Pete Carroll notes in his foreword to Tim Gallwey's classic *The Inner Game of Tennis* that "[t]he confidence necessary for performing at a championship level over long periods of time can only be developed on the practice field through repetition." If a stroke breaks down under pressure, odds are that you have not sufficiently learned and practiced it.

Get to the point where you internalize the motion so that you use it under pressure as well as at other times. In Kiegiel's words, "It is your normal visceral reaction that counts. If you can't perform it under pressure, then you haven't achieved this type of refined movement." You may know the stroke intellectually. You may be able to demonstrate the stroke to a group. You may be able to hit the stroke in practice and in drills. But if you haven't reached the level where you naturally hit the stroke irrespective of the moment, in a real sense you have not fully learned it.

Practice, practice, and practice more so that your movements and strokes are a part of you, so that you perform them no matter what the moment, so that fear and pressure become irrelevant. Then, you will have gone a long way to handle pressure.

Embrace each challenge you meet. You will almost never play your best against weaker opponents. Recognize that better opponents make you better. Rather than avoid or fear, adopt a "can do" attitude against everyone, especially the tougher opponents. Don't dwell on problems; instead search for solutions, *always*.

Practice, practice, and practice more. Repetitions and practice develop feel. Feel instills confidence. Confidence minimizes fear and anxiety.

Practice with pressure. Do drills where you put pressure on yourself. For instance, hit twenty overheads in a row without missing. If you miss, start again from zero and go until you reach twenty. Do the same with volleys deeper than the service line. On the serve, do the seven-serve drill, where you must hit seven consecutive flat serves in, seven consecutive kick/topspin serves in, and seven consecutive slice serves in. If you miss one, go back to zero, and keep going until you succeed.

As mentioned earlier, *everyone* gets nervous. *Everyone!* While your own nervousness and anxiety are unique to you, recognize that everyone, including your opponent, feels similarly at some times. Once you accept that pressure and anxiety happen to everyone, it is easier to accept, rather than deny or ignore, that they happen to you. Then, you can deal with it, intelligently and maturely.

One example of adapting to pressure in tennis is attributed to Hall of Famer and multiple Grand Slam champion Chris Evert. When nervous, Evert was known to continue to play relatively aggressively. She adapted to the pressure and nerves by continuing to hit hard but with more spin. When she got nervous, she tended to hit more through the middle of the court; she did not go for the lines. She continued to hit the shots she could hit; she just hit with more margin of error. By doing this, she adapted to the pressure and anxiety of the moment, continuing to perform well but managing her performance intelligently and maturely.

Other Sports

In baseball, a physically and mentally prepared hitter is not afraid of failure. Robson talks about hitters creating "presence" at the plate and keeping a positive "hitter's attitude." He says that the best hitters have the "attitude" but that they still respect their opponents.

While a .300 hitter is an all-star, the fact remains that a .300 hitter fails 70 percent of the time. In a close tennis match, the winning player will often lose almost 50 percent of the points. Whether in baseball or tennis, failure is an inherent part of the game.

Accept that failure is part of the game. Move on. Move on, staying in the present. Focus on "this pitch, this moment," "this ball, this moment."

In his book, Mike Malaska talks about a golf lesson he had with his coach Joe Nichols. In a playing lesson, after each shot by Malaska, Nichols would pick up and replace Malaska's ball in a more difficult spot, challenging Malaska to hit the more difficult shot. Malaska was pumped up for the challenge and played pretty well, considering the circumstances.

Afterward Nichols asked, "If, instead of me, you were the one who hit the shot into the bad place, would you have shot as well?" The same shot was in play, but the difference would have been that it was after a bad shot. Malaska thought that assuredly he would not have played as well. He would have been affected by the prior bad shot that gave him the bad lie. The normal golfer, rather than accept the challenge of the bad lie, normally lets the prior bad shot affect performance on the bad lie, thus adversely affecting his game even more. The lesson? Forget the prior shot; embrace positively the challenge before you. Get to where you can perform, meeting any challenge with enthusiasm, even when not playing well.

Malaska notes that the mental game and attitude are misunderstood and underappreciated. In golf, the dream is you enter some euphoric walk in nature, while the reality is every round will challenge you emotionally. How you deal with these challenges determines your success far more than your talent ever will. Achieving potential depends more on attitude rather than talent.

It is easy to be tough when you are playing well, not so much when you are not. True toughness rests with your gutting it out even when you are not at your best. In other words, when things are not going well, deal with it. Learn to love your demons. Learn to love pressure. Deal with it, and enjoy dealing with it. Embrace the challenge and figure out a way to make it work.

Malaska notes where golfers fail so many times is in their reaction to adversity. Golf is a game of emotions and adjustments. Reaction management is critical in all performance and competition. How you react often determines how you perform.

Koga asserts that in martial arts, "your most important attributes when you approach an explosive situation are your own self-confidence and self-control." Koga talks about self-defense, but his instructions also ring true for the attitude, clearheadedness, and balance required for other sports and tennis. If this relaxed mental alertness works in martial arts, it assuredly works elsewhere.

Golfer Tiger Woods, at the peak of his game, is one example of the kind of presence, control, and domination that pressured his opponents. Writer Jaime Diaz quoted Wood's fellow golfer J. C. Snead, who spoke of Wood's aura, domination, confidence, talent, and control: "He (Tiger) knew he was going to beat you; you knew he was going to beat you; and he knew you knew he was gonna beat you." At his peak, opponents seemingly wilted in the presence of Tiger Woods. They pushed and pressured themselves beyond their limits simply because they had to compete against Tiger. As a result, many players played worse against Tiger because of his presence, control, and pressure.

Another example of dominating and pressuring opponents lies with competitive long-distance running. Often the way to win a race when in the lead pack is to pick up the pace just a little, perhaps a second or two per mile/kilometer. Then, when the others adjust to the increased pace, increase the speed another second or two per mile/kilometer. Then do it again and again and again. Each increment puts just a bit more pressure on the racers. After a while, runners start to fall off from the increased pace, and many, when they fall off, don't just adjust down to the next lower level; they slow down dramatically. In other words, they "break." From the leader's perspective, the broken runners don't just gradually fade back; they disappear. Not only does the gradually cumulative pressure overly strain their bodies, it also breaks their will to the point they no longer fully compete.

Too often you miss the thrill of the unexpected by forcing every shot and every outcome to conform to your expectations. Rather than expect this, deal with and embrace the uncertainty. Don't waste the chance to learn how to deal with the unexpected, including the emotional challenges of the game and life.

Keeping a great attitude is important throughout training as well as competition. Face it. You spend so much more time training than competing that if you don't love practice and training, you're going to be in for a tough, long, hard slog. Mastery of anything only comes with practice and sound fundamentals. Learn to love practice and the process. Learn to love everything.

Beginning this chapter is Mark Beede's poem "Compete." To summarize and emphasize, we repeat:

Compete
Compete with attitude.
Compete confidently.
Compete fearlessly.
Enjoy the battle, win or lose.
Welcome pressure.
Embrace pressure.
Compete . . . now.

CHAPTER FOUR

CONCENTRATION AND STAYING IN THE PRESENT

Concentration is a skill developed through learning and practice, like any other technique. Learn to stay in the present. Almost always something tempts you to take your mind away from the now. Accept that you're not perfect; everyone's mind wanders. When you realize you are not in the present, whether you are dwelling in the past on what just happened or worrying about what will happen, just bring your mind back to the now and what needs doing now. Don't dwell on the past. Don't worry about the future. *Focus on now!*

What we are talking about is a kind of "peephole concentration," which means focusing on the task or event completely while ignoring the irrelevant noise, confusion, and chaos around. Peephole concentration removes confusion and distraction. Martial artists sometimes talk about going from "soft" focus to "hard" focus. Soft focus allows one to take in the general situation and circumstances before the critical moment; however, just before the critical time of attack or defense, one narrows to hard focus by keying on the point of greatest threat. Hard focus, while exceptionally useful for perception, also keeps one concentrated and in the present.

The Eastern outlook focuses more on the process and journey than the ultimate result. The advantage of focusing on the process places the player more in the moment. Rather than focusing on consequences, one instead focuses on one's actions as he performs them; in other words, one focuses on the *present*. What you are doing right *now* is the focus. It is the *doing* that is important, not the results of the doing. Do now!

Thinking of consequences necessarily takes one out of the present by thinking of the future, of what will happen if this or that happens now. Thinking of consequences literally puts a historical perspective on what is happening now. Thinking of history, how now relates to the present and the past in terms of results, displaces focus from the present and impedes performance.

The present, the here and now, is the important focus. It is this focus on the present and process that is integral to Asian philosophy. The Western view, with its emphasis on results, distracts one from the present while producing anxiety and pressure, factors that in themselves block flow, performance, and achievement.

Focus primarily on process, that is to say, present performance, and ideally, there is no need to worry about results. In a sense, this is a bit of a trick, because results remain ultimately important if someone is keeping score with an eye to finishing the game with a win or a loss. However, if you concern or worry yourself primarily about the ultimate goal rather than simply dealing with the present, assuredly your performance will suffer.

In fighting, stay in the moment; don't think or worry about the result. If you fight and think "I may die," the chances increase dramatically that you will die.[2]

Keep in the present, and results take care of themselves. Take yourself out of the present by worrying about the result, worrying about winning and losing, and fear and anxiety will creep in, hindering performance.

---

[2] Clearly this is speculative, given the obvious difficulties in confirming or researching a fighter's thoughts immediately before dying in battle. "What were you thinking just before he killed you?" obviously is an impossible question to substantiate. However, we stand by our assertion to concentrate in the present and that worrying about the result impedes performance.

Tennis

Tennis provides so many opportunities and potential distractions to take one out of the moment, out of the *now*. For instance, by not playing as if each point is match point, one tends to play the score. Don't play the score. Everyone has mental letups and lapses, especially after long games and service breaks. When you feel your mind wander, and everyone's does, just think how you will play the next point. Don't get down on yourself; don't tell yourself to concentrate. Actually telling yourself to concentrate admits that you're not concentrating, and chiding yourself to do so still keeps you out of the moment. Rather than berating yourself to concentrate, just focus on how to play the next point; and do that *now*.

Where your eyes are, your mind is. When playing or practicing, keep your eyes on the task at hand. Usually there is no need to look around off the court when playing. Help yourself stay focused by keeping your eyes on the court. When feeling as if you want to wander, look at your racket. Develop rituals that keep you focused, such as focusing on the strings between each point. Keep your eyes, and therefore your mind, on the court and the ball. Switch from soft focus to hard focus on the ball when your opponent strokes the ball and again when the ball bounces on your side of the court.

Don't get caught up playing personalities. Worrying about the person on the other side of the net, whether he bothers you or is trying to bother you, only distracts from the primary objective at hand. Stay calm. Play the match. Stay focused on the *now* of playing the point.

Play each point as if it is match point. While easier said than done, playing each point as if it is the ultimate point helps you play in the *now*. Because *now* is the most important time to perform, playing each point with the intensity of match point helps you to intensify the *now*. Play each point as if it is match point, *because each point is the most important point at the time it is played.* By playing *now*, by becoming immersed in the moment with the present point as the most important point, you go a long way to complete concentration.

Concentration wins matches. Concentration separates players of equal ability. Don't worry about the past or the future; *now* is the only time that matters. Take care of the present. Do everything possible to win the point *now*. Play the point *now* as if it is the only one you want. Then do it again.

Letting go is the highest level of sport. Don't fear the results. Engage in the process. Work to set up and hit targets. Work to set up and hit targets *now*, irrespective of the score or the moment.

Concentration is being in the present, in the *now*. Don't force it, just relax and play *now*.

Other Sports

In golf, Malaska repeatedly admonishes to just play one shot at a time. Stay in the present; don't focus on anything else.

In baseball, Robson coaches players to always think, "This pitch, this moment." Robson also referred to former all-star pitcher Sam McDowell, who pitched according to "this pitch, this moment." "This pitch, this moment" simply means you're focusing all your energy and attention on what is about to happen, nothing more. "This pitch, this moment" means the peephole concentration mentioned before. For the hitter, "this pitch, this moment" means going from soft focus to hard focus or peephole concentration by focusing on the pitcher's arm socket, arm, hand, and ball.

It doesn't matter whether you are a hitter, a pitcher, a golfer, or a tennis player. Focus on this pitch or this ball this moment and nothing else. Become oblivious to extraneous matters like people in the stands, the need to move runners along, whether you are in position to hit a winner, or whether you have match point.

"I have to hit or else," "Don't screw up," "What happens if I strike out?" "If I win the next point, I win the match"—these are all thoughts *not* in the moment. Think instead, "This pitch, this moment," "This ball, this moment."

The mentally tough take responsibility for their thoughts and attempt to maintain consistency, which is reflected by their actions and results. Consistency comes from learning to play the game one pitch, stroke, or shot at a time, whether the game is baseball, golf, or tennis.

According to Robson, a hitting slump in baseball usually results from mental mistakes more than physical ones. Stay in the present. What has happened in the past is over and done with. What is about to happen is the only thing that matters. This pitch, this moment; this stroke, this moment; this shot, this moment.

When talking about baseball, Robson says that mental preparation consists of clearing the mind of all negative thoughts and being able to focus. Is there any sport or athletic endeavor where this doesn't apply? Concentration is fundamental.

Remember:
Love the moment.
Do now.
Be now.

CHAPTER FIVE

CALMNESS AND RELAXATION

By focusing on the process, on the present, on what you are doing right *now*, you help yourself relax. Once you relax, you flow and move from one move to the next without tightness, without pressure.

Power is elusive. The more you try for power, the more it disappears. Tension destroys power. Instead, counterintuitively, relax to gain power.

Former Wimbledon champion Goran Ivanisevic, a powerful server, is reputed to have noted this with his serve. When Ivanisevic tried to hit a big serve, his serve actually got slower! Upon realizing and learning this, he relaxed to keep his serve big.

Tension manifests itself in the upper body, arms, and hands. Think of the legs and lower body controlling the upper body, arms, and hands. Think of the legs and lower body as the aggressors, as the real workers, while keeping the arms and hands as relaxed, almost passive followers.

Confusion increases the time it takes for evaluation, for reaching conclusions, and for reaction by the body. Discipline your mind to remain calm and flexible at all times, and you reduce your own reaction lag time. Remaining calm and flexible at all times with peephole concentration prevents distractions from disturbing your thoughts and affecting your actions.

Because a relaxed mind is unfettered and flexible, one's reaction to sudden emergency quickens. Aside from any specific techniques they may know, this neutral concentration and instantaneous reaction is what makes real experts in judo, jujitsu, aikido, and karate so formidable.

A key principle of natural law, relaxation allows for fluid motion, coordinated motion, and a clear mind. Without relaxation, motion suffers, timing suffers, and thinking is clouded. An ironclad rule in martial arts training is, rigidity is the ultimate enemy of fluid movement. Certainly it is the ultimate enemy of your transition from loading to unloading your strike. Relax for results.

As mentioned earlier, calm, relaxed, peephole concentration prevents confusion and distractions from affecting your actions. If these principles apply to disciplines, which revolve around self-defense and survival, they surely apply to other sports, such as baseball, golf, and tennis, mere games of hitting a ball.

In golf, Kiegiel talks about "rounding," which is relaxing throughout the body rather than tensing. Another analogy is the oblivious drunkard who is so relaxed that he remains impervious to injury from his inebriated accidents.

To practice relaxing, try the visualization/meditation exercise in chapter 8. You'll find that you'll feel better, focus better, and play better.

Remember:
Relax the body and the mind.
Learn, and be aware where and when you tighten up.
Relax in those situations.
Stay calm and relaxed, emotionally and in the body.
Relaxation comes from and allows
ying and yang,
flow and force.

CHAPTER SIX

YING AND YANG: FLOW AND FORCE

Focusing on the present with relaxation and flow leads to a clear and quiet mind, calm emotions, confidence, and with sufficient practice, fearlessness.

To the traditional Western-trained athlete, martial arts carry almost a mystical, magical, exotic aura. Supporting this mystical art are the flowing terms *ying*, *yang*, and *ki*. What are they?

In *Striking Thoughts*, Bruce Lee, also a former philosophy student, noted that the Taoist Chinese conceived the entire universe as activated by two principles, yang and ying, and that nothing exists except by the interplay of the two forces. Matter and energy, yang and ying, heaven and earth, are thought of as essentially one or as two coexistent poles of one indivisible whole.

The ying and yang connect the active with the passive, the flow with strength and force. Inextricably connected, ying and yang work together to produce a relaxed flow of power.[3] "The universal balance of life," ying is nature's passive energy, while yang is forceful energy. While one thinks of yang as force, ying is any energy that yields.

Add to these terms *ki*, which is the one source from which power flows, the "one point" from which one summons reserves of power and emotional strength, and we are in the East. Some refer to the ki one point as an actual place in the body, slightly

---

[3] Bruce Lee, in *Striking Thoughts*, said that *ying-yang* is not two things, but instead poles of one interconnected process. Given this, he said that one should not use the word *and* when discussing or considering them (yet he does so in another place). Whether we use *ying-yang* or *ying and yang*, it is useful to understand them as two parts of an interconnected process, while also recognizing that neither can be omitted nor separate from the other.

below the navel. Most keep their athletic balance higher than their ki one point. Simply by lowering your core athletic center of gravity to your ki one point will probably improve your performance.

Utilizing your central power source, your ki with your movements' ying and yang, produces a relaxed flow from the center of balance, producing amazing acceleration and power. The simple martial arts approach of ying, yan, and ki utilizes natural law, that is to say, actual physics, to unlock one's natural powers. Ying, yang, ki, ground force, and other Eastern principles naturally turn you into a better athlete in whatever you do. The natural law (or physics) of body alignments and rotation, along with relaxation, directs countless movements on and off the martial arts mat.

In golf, Kiegiel talks about a 1-2-3 rhythm, with 1 for the backswing, 2 for the unloading and impact, and 3 for the follow-through. As players approach the professional level, the rhythm changes slightly so that steps 2 and 3 occur almost simultaneously.

In tennis, the same type of rhythm and flow apply. For instance, with the ground stroke, the 1-2-3 rhythm applies with 1 for the load, 2 for the unload and stroke through the ball, and 3 for the follow-through. There is a different flow to the serve, but a flow nonetheless. Toss and extend the arm with a slow 1-2 count and then explode fast up into and through the ball on the 3 count. With the serve, think slow-slow-fast.

On the return of serve, with fastballs, fast deep balls, volleys, and balls hit at your feet, go with a 1-2 flow rather than the normal 1-2-3 rhythm. On these harder, faster balls, still keep the rhythm and flow going, just shorten the stroke and the count to allow for the quicker time. These situations are similar to what Kiegiel notes with professional golfers in that the normal rhythm is shortened with the normal 2-3 rhythm occurring almost simultaneously, compressing into almost a single count.

Martial arts and the Eastern philosophy of ying and yang apply to golf, to tennis, and perhaps to all sports. Kiegiel suggests the following ying and yang rhythm to the golf stroke:

Setup—ying
Backswing—yang
Top of backswing to transition—ying
Downswing, impact, and follow-through—yang
Finish—ying

The same applies to the tennis stroke. Loading is the initial yang, with the finished load the ying; the unloading through the ball is the yang, with the follow-through flowing back through the ying.

Ying and yang provide flow and tempo. Feel the flow. Feel the tempo. As you do this, you will feel the timing of your stroke, whether in golf or in tennis.

Martial arts, golf, baseball, tennis, and other striking sports involve synchronization of body parts taking energy from the ground, utilizing the kinetic chain to transfer that energy into an object. What's the most important part of that synchronization? Ying and yang, timing and flow.

Remember:
Flow from your ki,
the center of balance just below your navel.
Feel the ying and yang,
the flow and force.

CHAPTER SEVEN

BREATHING

Breathing is normal and essential. Everyone breathes, but some breathe better than others. Believe it or not, proper breathing is fundamental to high performance. Not everyone breathes properly or optimally. Breathe properly, and you'll help yourself relax and achieve flow, infusing your body with oxygen to fuel your body, while eliminating waste product, such as carbon dioxide and other waste.

When nervous or excited, people tend to breathe fast and shallow, breathing only from their upper lungs. By not utilizing their lung's full capacity, they inhibit their body's ability to fully oxygenize, creating weakness and fatigue while limiting performance.

Relaxed, calm people tend to breathe more slowly and deeply.

Learn to breathe deeply even when competing. Learn to use all your lungs, not just a portion of them. We need oxygen to compete; heck, we need oxygen to live. Let's work to fulfill our body's full potential by ensuring we take in as much oxygen as possible.

Breathe from your diaphragm, centering yourself. Breathing from the diaphragm helps keep you calm, relaxed, and centered. Often, when fighters and athletes get excited, they breathe more and more shallow. Instead, keep breathing from the diaphragm, from the center, and you'll naturally relax.

One useful almost meditative breathing exercise is to focus on breathing in seven counts. First, inhale in seven distinct counts, focusing on filling your lungs with air, then hold for a count of seven. Then, exhale in seven distinct counts, contracting your diaphragm and expelling the air from your lungs. Hold for another count of seven. Then inhale again, repeating the process.

If a seven count is too much, try the same exercise but with fewer counts. As you get used to the exercise over time, increase the counts beyond seven to whatever you can. Focus on your breathing; focus on the air entering and leaving your lungs. You will find that this exercise relaxes and centers you. Do this regularly as part of your normal routine to help stay centered and relaxed.

When on the court, after a stressful point, try the same exercise, but instead go with a four count, given the time limitations. Slow down. Breathe from the center. On the changeover, feel free to put a towel over your head and do the same four-count exercise.

Remember:
Breathe from the bottom of the diaphragm.
Breathe between points and on changeovers.
Breathe deeply
to
still the mind
and
relax.

CHAPTER EIGHT

CONNECTEDNESS AND VISUALIZATION THE MIND AND BODY AS ONE

All the factors we've talked about work together to form a connectedness, a oneness consisting of the physical, mental, emotional, and spiritual. Within the physical, there is a purely physical connectedness that consists of the biomechanical connectors, the kinetic chain emanating from the ground, which we cover later in chapter 12. But for now, we examine the entire mind and body working together in harmony.

Balance and equilibrium remain essential to connect the mind, body, and spirit. We can consider balance and equilibrium in a purely physical sense, but we can also think of it as inherent in combining the physical with the mental and emotional. Balance is not just physically standing on your feet without falling; balance also includes body and mind.

Kiegiel sees the concept of clear movement through a clear mind as at the heart of the martial arts. "The mind leads the body." Any anxiety, anger, or frustration, even too much excitement, will slow and affect you. Get to the point of "mind of no mind" or what the Japanese refer to as *mushin*. Achieving *mushin* is the ultimate. By attaining a mind of no thought, one responds instinctively with flow, fully utilizing the power of ying and yang. Some dojos call this mental state *unattachment*.

The mind and body are one. The two are never neutral. If the mind and body fail to work together, they conflict. One cannot divorce the mind from the body, and vice versa. Strive to become unattached, to attain *mushin*, "a mind of no mind." Make your body and mind one, but without your ego. Detach your ego from your performance; allow yourself to flow.

Imagery/Visualization

While achieving *mushin*, a mind of no mind, is the ultimate in executing with flow, prior to action, the mind plays an important, almost controlling role in preconditioning the body to action, and anticipating through imaging or visualizing. Visualization or imaging is a way of rehearsing, of being ready for what actually happens. Visualization and imaging help connect the mind and the body.

Where the mind is, the body goes. Visualization or imaging is the means of using the "mind's eye" to precondition one to anticipate something or to execute a shot. In the book *Smart Tennis: How to Play and Win the Mental Game*, John Murray says that imagery helps prepare strategies, rehearse shot sequences, and improve timing and placement by organizing a mental plan for performance. Through visualization and imagery, you simulate reality. Imagining what you will do in a certain circumstance readies you for and helps anticipate a particular event.

The noted sports psychologist James Loehr, in *Mental Toughness Training for Sports: Achieving Athletic Excellence*, says that we are like image-sensitive computers. The mental images we have about what we can and can't do determine how we respond and act. Images serve as roadmaps. "If you program in negative and self-defeating images, that's precisely what you'll get back in performance."

To engender success, develop a positive roadmap. As Loehr says, "visualization is . . . the . . . practice of creating and strengthening strong, positive mental images," and it is dramatically effective for translating desire into physical performance.

In his seminal best-selling book *Psycho-Cybernetics*, Dr. Maxwell Maltz asserts that the brain is incapable of distinguishing between something that actually happened from something vividly imagined. If you can imagine something vividly, it's as if it has actually happened.

This is strong stuff when used correctly. As Loehr says, "thinking it paves the way to doing it!" Rather than telling yourself to do something, picture yourself doing it. Then, copy the image in reality.

Visualization or imagery is not a delusionary exercise or a trip into irrelevant fantasy. Visualization or imagery is rather an important, essential tool for the elite athlete. Murray believes that elite athletes use imagery and visualization more often than average athletes and that imagery and success go hand in hand.

Pointing to golfing great Jack Nicklaus, NFL star quarterback Fran Tarkenton, and Olympic decathlon gold medalist Bruce Jenner (now Caitlyn Jenner) as successful visualization practitioners, Loehr asserts that visualization is a fundamental and important exercise for every serious athlete. Loehr claims Nicklaus attributes 50 percent of his success to visualization. Loehr also quotes Jenner as claiming that his daily mental rehearsal substantially helped him win his Olympic gold medal.

If the testimonies of athletic greats Nicklaus, Tarkenton, Jenner, and numerous other elite athletes are not enough, consider Australian psychologist Alan Richardson's experiment with basketball. Richardson had his subjects each shoot one hundred free throws. After recording the results, he then divided his participants into three separate groups. The first group then returned to the basketball court to practice actual free throws for twenty minutes a day, five days a week for four weeks. The second group was told not to do anything basketball related for four weeks, including not even thinking about basketball. The third group came to the basketball court and, with the aid of a visualization coach, visualized and imagined shooting free throws, *without touching a basketball.*

After four weeks, each subject shot another one hundred actual shots. Those in the first group, the ones who had actually practiced foul shots, improved 24%. Not surprisingly, those who had not practiced at all, did not improve significantly. Interestingly, the third group, the visualization group, improved 23%, almost as much as the group that had actually practiced!

While many use the term *visualization* to describe the concept at hand, the more accurate term might be *imagery*, as the concept applies to more than just visual imagining. Imagery also applies to nonvisual senses, such as feelings, sensations, emotions, sounds, and other senses. For athletic performance, kinesthetic and visual markers are probably the most relevant. Think of mental simulation of the various senses for the words *imagery* or *visualization.*

Just as airplane pilots use flight simulators to practice flying, use your mind to simulate practice, playing, and competing. Mental imagery takes many forms, including visual, kinesthetic, or aural simulations. You can visualize or "see" you performing. You can imagine feeling calm and relaxed in a circumstance. What works best for one may differ from another. Some, particularly visual learners, may "see" or visualize better, while others, such as kinesthetic learners, may "feel" more.

Visualize or imagine changing a bad habit into a good one. For instance take a stroke that needs improving and imagine the correct picture or feeling, or both.

"See" the shot. "Feel" the shot, staying composed throughout—before, during and after. Imagine yourself stroking the ball to your target without your head turning to watch it land. Imagine trusting in your shot.

Make the picture or feeling as realistic as you can. You'll find that as you practice imaging, you'll develop the ability to simulate pictures and feelings more and more realistically. Try to work the complete picture and full feeling into your imaging, including the "correct" psychological states of confidence, focus, attitude, calmness, and relaxation. While this may be difficult at first, with practice you will develop more and more complete images including the visual and kinesthetic.

"Change" a past loss into a win. Imagine a prior loss, and examine what went wrong. Then imagine performing the correct movement or feeling at the critical time. For instance, you may have double-faulted into the net by dropping your head and pulling down. Imagine yourself in the situation hitting the second serve correctly by driving up the body and racket while keeping the head up.

While this technique certainly doesn't change the actual past, imagery helps you learn from your mistakes and your past, which in turn helps you prepare for the future, increasing your chances of performing successfully the next time you meet the similar situation.

For future events, imagine yourself with the correct attitude, calmness, focus, concentration, and presence. Imagine yourself hitting your shots, moving and setting up with balance. Imagine yourself flowing through your shots. Imagine yourself strong.

Imagine correct technique, which means you need to know correct technique. Murray says, "Garbage in, garbage out."

Imagine and simulate the right stuff; your body follows your mind. Make sure your mind provides the right direction.

To develop anticipation, before a point, imagine a particular shot sequence. For instance, imagine you're serving a first serve in and then moving into the court to hit a forehand, taking advantage of the point. Visualizing like this familiarizes you with high-percentage shot sequences and helps develop anticipation skills for quicker and more effective responses.

After a match or performance, pick out what you did best and image those aspects. Thinking and imaging successful shots, successful performance, and good feelings reinforce good habits and actions, which in turn develop implicit flow and improved performance.

Imagine a future performance, keeping in mind only positive feelings and actions. Imagine your ideal states of performance. Visualizing and imaging of the future with positive pictures and feelings help provide a positive plan leading to an ideal state of flowing performance.

Keep your visualizing and imaging realistic. Imagine active movement and balance. It is unrealistic to imagine hitting 150-mile-per-hour second serve aces into the wide corner. In this regard, as contradictory as it may seem, keep your fantasies real. As Murray notes, to produce maximum benefits, imagery content should be technically precise, clear, vivid, controllable, and realistic.

When visualizing, how do you see yourself? Some see themselves from the outside, as if they were actors in a movie and they were watching the movie. It is this type of visualization that Murray refers to as external imagery and Loehr refers to as objective visualization. Others visualize as if they were looking through their own eyes to the outside world, which Loehr refers to as subjective visualization and Murray as internal imagery.

Both perspectives are useful. For improving technique, often the external perspective helps the player see himself from the outside and visualize corrections to the entire body. The internal or subjective perspective is more helpful for handling the entire circumstance of a point and imaging feelings, sensations, and emotions. Generally, we believe that the internal perspective is preferred as, to quote Gallwey, "natural learning always comes from the inside out, not vice versa."

In connecting the mind and body as one, the Westerner may think of the word *psychosomatic*, a word which in some circles carries a negative connotation. Not so here! Here, psychosomatic is *positively* essential.

Psychosomatic is not some psychological nerd-driven piece of meaningless mumbo jumbo. Psychosomatics are real, in that the mind and emotions control the body.

As Loehr says, "visualization is not magic and does not take the place of hard, physical practice. There is no substitute for physical practice, but physical practice wins only half the battle. Thinking in positive pictures wins the other half."

A Visualization/Meditation Tennis Exercise

As a specific exercise to visualize and mediate for tennis, try the following:

> *First, lie down*
> *Your arms by your side*
> *Now tighten your whole body*
> *Tighten your hands*

Tighten your arms
Chest
Legs
Feet
Buttocks
Facial muscles
Hinges of the jaw
Continue to breathe
Tighten as much as you can
15 seconds
10
5
4
3
2
1
Now relax
Listen to your breathing
Slow, rhythmical breathing
Listen to your breathing
Use all your senses
Breathe from the bottom of the diaphragm
Feel your body relax into the ground beneath you
Relax everything
Your legs
Your feet
Your toes
Your arms
Your hands
Your fingers
Your stomach
Your buttocks
Your facial muscles
Everything
But keep breathing

Relax everything
10 more seconds
9
8
7
6
Everything
5
4
3
2
1
Relax
Listen to your breathing
Each time you exhale, listen to the air as it leaves your body
Feel the energy drain from your body
Feel all ten toes relax
Let your feet start to relax
Your ankles
Let the calves go
Around the knees, start to relax
Listen to your breathing
Let the hamstrings go
The quadriceps
Now let your legs and buttocks start to sink into the ground
Start to feel as if you couldn't move from the waist down even if you wanted to
Listen to your breathing
Every time you exhale, it's energy leaving
Sinking into the ground
Let all ten fingers relax.
Feel them
Your little fingers
Ring fingers
Index fingers

Thumbs
Feel all your fingers relax, the tension leaving
Let the wrists start to go
Let the forearms relax
Around the elbows
Feel the biceps relaxing
And triceps
Gravity is pulling the shoulders back into the ground
Feel from the shoulders down to the legs that
you couldn't move even if you wanted to
All the energy is draining from your body
Listen to your breathing as you exhale
Actually listen to the sound of the air as it leaves your body
Sinking
Start to let your neck muscles relax
Let the hinges of the jaw relax
Let your facial muscles relax
Feel as if gravity is pulling the cheeks back
As you exhale, you are sinking
Feel as if you are on an escalator, going down ten stairs
Every stair down, relax a little more
9th level
8
7
Continue to listen to your breathing as you exhale
6
5
4
3
2
1
You're on the bottom level
Absolutely relaxed
No energy in the body, physical . . . or mental
You're just sinking

*Your body feels totally heavy
You couldn't move your arms or your body if you wanted to*

*Go to your favorite place in the world
It doesn't matter where
A beach
Your house
Your bed
The forest
Your favorite place in the world
And you're totally relaxed*

*Now think of tennis
Forehands
Think of setting up to hit down the line
Your shoulders are turned
Your hips are turned
You're hitting the ball in your power zone
It doesn't matter whether you're in the
middle of the court or on the alley,
You're setting up to hit down the line
Let the ball get into your contact zone
You're hitting off the back leg
You're throwing the racket right over the net at
a certain zone, either low, middle, or high
Hit the ball between your feet
Keeping balance before, during, and after
Hit some backhands that way
The TV commentators are saying, "Gee, he looks
as if he is hitting down the line, moving forward,
ready to come to net every single time"
See the racket head whipping around the
outside of the ball as you're so loose
It's all back leg and hip rotation*

Feel the racket whipping around the ball
Your eyes staying where the ball is, not where it's going
Now hit some crosscourts
Your opponent is going to be late, because you're so
good an actor showing you're hitting down the line

Your opponent is now coming to net to volley
Imagine you're hitting low through zone one
Imagine the deep balls to you
Keeping the racket handle down and stroking right back at him
Loose fingers
The racket is lagging and whipping
Accelerating
On the short ball, you're pouncing and
stopping, rotating through the ball

Your opponent is at net
If it's deep, you're level
If it's shorter, you tilt,
Hitting off the back leg
Back low through zone one
Handle down
You never rush, because no one in the world can read you

Run around and stroke some inside-out forehands
With the same setup, hit some lobs
Over the opponent's head
Hit to a target
See the arc

You can go down the line, crosscourt, or lob
Same rhythm
Same setup
Champion's composure
They're moving back

You're moving to the net
Every volley is through the court
Your back is straight
Racket straight through the ball, just as with the ground strokes
All legs
Turn your chest, setting up to volley down the line
But you decide where to volley
Down the line
Through the middle
Crosscourt
Deep
Angle
Same set up
Same rhythm
Same look
You're like a wall; the harder he hits, the more
you sit down and play it back deep

Move closer to the net
All volleys
Deep
Angles
Drop shots
Same setup
Same rhythm
Same look

No one in the world can tell the difference
between what you're going to do.

Hit some overheads
The ball is up
Lower your center
Get your head in line
Step in with the front foot

The ball's coming right down on your forehead
You're down low
The ball goes up and you lower
Set up
Set up
Relax
And tap up on the ball
Don't look at them; look at the ball

Now you're playing doubles
Your partner's is serving and you're volleying
Take pride on every ball that hits the net, as your hips are turned
Your spine perpendicular with your shoulders,
spine straight up and down
Hitting through the center of the court
Staying balanced through the finish, no falling or stepping

Return of serve—all serves: kick serves, flat serves, slice serves
Perpendicular
Your hips are turned
You're hitting level
Catch
Turn the hips
Turn the hips
Turn the hips

Now some serves
Warm up your slice
See the ball lifting
As your racket lifts up and around the ball
How loose is your arm
Don't look at the ball; see it in your mind's eye where it's going

All lower body
Upper body is loose

Hit some kicks
Hit the left side of the ball (for righties)

The more you hit up, the shorter the ball lands
The shorter it lands, the more it bounces off the court

Don't worry about your opponent.
Hit your target and he's helpless.

Now flat serves
Eighty percent pace flat serves
Hit some targets

Now, go to a match that means a lot to you
When you were a really tough competitor
You had a reason
You fought your tail off
You found a way to get it done

Relive the last moments
Feel the feeling

Now to finish
Focus on your breathing
Your eyes closed
Slow, rhythmical breathing from the bottom of
the diaphragm up through the throat
Each deep breath, feel the energy return
into your arms, legs, and body

Listen to the air enter your body as you inhale
Literally energy returning to the body

*You may want to stay in the relaxed state, but it's
time to get back on the escalator and return*

*First level
Up to the 2nd
Listen to your breathing as you move
To the 3rd level
4th
5th level, more awake
6th
7th
8th
9th
and you're at the top
Step off the escalator with your eyes still closed*

*The energy is there
Brand-new day
Energy in your arms and legs
Two more deep breaths from the diaphragm through the throat
Feeling wide awake*

*Eyes closed
Now actually reach your arms over your
head and stretch your arms
Reach with your legs
Now get up and go.*

To make the mind and body one, you must study and practice. You cannot ignore either. Theory and practice go hand in hand. Make the mind and body one.

Is there any sport or activity where these precepts don't apply? No. This connectedness is fundamental and must exist for one to realize one's full potential.

Remember:
Mentally "see" or "feel" yourself
stroking
and reacting
correctly in every situation.
Imagine yourself committing mentally and physically,
before, during, and after,
to every shot and every point.

CHAPTER NINE

SIMPLICITY

Good techniques are simple techniques. Eliminate the extraneous. Focus on the core principles and core techniques. With simplicity comes conservation of energy, with energy focused into one place. At the top levels, things become simpler and seemingly easier.

Maximum force out of minimum motion, or pure ying and yang—that's what it is all about. Simplicity of movement, the rule of martial arts is the very core of success.

Keep it simple. So much of the game is simple, yet too many fighters and tennis players overcomplicate. Keep it simple, but how does one simplify? The solution lies with footwork, movement, and balance. The key to simplicity comes with movement. Work hard to make it easy.

Earlier we've said that if you feel rushed hitting a shot, you're probably hitting the wrong shot. If you feel rushed, simplify. Shorten the stroke, put the racket on the ball, and back into play.

Stay within yourself; keep it simple, doing what you *know* you can do, not what you *think* you can do.

In tennis particularly, move your feet so that you can make the shot simple. Keep it simple; eliminate unnecessary movement.

Remember:
The higher the level, the simpler the action.

CHAPTER TEN

ANTICIPATION, PERCEPTION, AND REACTION

In the old days, just as players and coaches ignored the nonphysical intangibles, they also ignored the critical link between perceiving and reacting. Even today, the tendency is to focus solely on acting without regard to anticipating, seeing, and reacting. Even when the question was raised before, the answer often was that the ability to anticipate, see, perceive, and react is innate and fixed. How wrong this is! Not only are anticipation, vision, perception, and reaction important, one can improve in each area!

Tennis, martial arts, and baseball are examples of open skills perception sports. In each sport, you must anticipate, see, and perceive well; then you need to react quickly to employ your skill sets whether in fighting, stroking a tennis ball, or hitting a baseball.

Balls move fast on a big tennis court, and time is limited. With an advanced player, the ball takes about 0.4 seconds to travel from one end of the court to another. A player needs 0.3 to 0.5 seconds to move into position. Obviously, there is not a lot of extra time to see and decide what to do. Therefore, the faster and better one can anticipate, see, and perceive, the more time one has to react and dictate, and the better one can perform.

Anticipation

Anticipation is the act of foreseeing or predicting an event. We're not talking about extrasensory perception (ESP) here; we're talking about sensory perception. Anticipation allows one to predict the future by utilizing various cues to determine what a ball or opponent will do.

Anticipation is the act of predicting a future event. The better one anticipates, readies himself for, and expects an occurrence, the better one perceives what is happening when it happens. Anticipation and perception are intertwined; the better you anticipate, the sooner you'll perceive what's happening. Similarly, the better you perceive, the better you anticipate what will happen next.

There are different types of anticipation. For instance, one can perceive a ball's flight, spin, and pace and from that anticipate where the ball will land and how it will bounce. Also, a player may perceive what his opponent does and does not do in particular circumstances, and anticipate his opponent's reaction to a particular situation in light of that history. Additionally, by seeing where an opponent is on the court, one can often anticipate what type of shot his opponent will hit, whether offensive, neutral, or defensive. Knowing the geometry of the court allows one to know which effective shots are available and, just as importantly, which are not. Also, by seeing or perceiving such other cues as an opponent's balance, footwork or lack of footwork, and grips, one acquires information to more accurately predict his opponent's shot.

Readiness for the Greatest Threat

We have said that the better one anticipates, readies himself for, and expects an occurrence, the better he perceives what is happening when it happens. A basic anticipatory precept: *Ready yourself for the greatest threat.*

Ready yourself for the greatest threat. Look for the greatest threat first, and go from there. What does the greatest threat mean? In fighting, it often means looking to your opponent's leg and arm that are closest to you, as those are the two with the immediate greatest danger as they can strike you more quickly. In baseball, it means looking for the fastball first. In tennis, it means looking for the hardest and fastest shot first.

In fighting, always train and compete by readying for the quickest attack. We call this "training for the fastball," as in baseball. If you ready yourself for the quickest attack, you have time for a slower approach. Conversely, if you train or ready yourself for a slower attack, you will not be ready for the quick strike. Get ready for the quick strike, and you'll have time to defend against a slower attack. In this sense, always "train for the fastball."

- For instance, in fighting a right-handed opponent, look to the left foot and left hand; they are the closest to you and will be the first to strike as they will get to you the quickest. If you are not ready, your eyes, groin, or knees are taken out! You have more time to defend against the right.

- Always be ready to move forward, whether in fighting or tennis.

Train for the fastball in tennis. While you want to take time away from your opponent, expect your opponent to do the same and train for the fastball. If you approach your setup and stroke in this fashion, you maximize your chances to be ready and to effectively respond. It is immeasurably easier to set up for a fastball, only to react to a slow ball, than it is to slowly prepare and have to react to a fastball. Be ready. Set up soon. Get balanced. Stroke.

In baseball, Robson coaches to always be ready for the fastball. "Early timing is better than late timing." If the hitter starts too early, he can always slow down; on the other hand, if a hitter starts too late, he cannot make up for lost time. A hitter must always be on time for the pitcher's fastest pitch. Tony Gwynn and Ted Williams, two of the best hitters of all time, trained themselves for the fastball. Training for the fastball still allows time for the changeups, curveballs, knuckleballs, and other pitches.

Additional anticipatory information comes from knowing your opponent. What shots does he like and not like? What are his strengths and weaknesses? What kind of shots does he hit under pressure? Scouting and knowing your opponent provides more information for the present, allowing you to be ready to accurately perceive what happens.

Vision

Sight and vision is the acuity one registers with an eye chart. Often one improves performance simply by getting his eyes checked and obtaining corrective lenses. It seems self-evident to assert that the better one can see, the better one perceives; however, many simply assume that their vision is adequate and not a performance limiting factor. Clearer vision produces better performance.

Perception

Perception is how well the brain interprets the signals the eye sees along with other senses, including sound and feel. Perceptual skill is fundamental to successful performance in fastball sports, such as tennis and baseball, as well as in martial arts and fighting disciplines. Perception plays an important role in response time, hand-body coordination, balance, spatial orientation, and anticipation, all of which affect performance. Tennis players have to perceive and interpret information quickly and effectively, to provide sufficient time to plan, initiate, and execute appropriate shots. Time constraints in tennis require one to process visual and other sensory information and react in fractions of a second.

Beginners tend to perceive relevant visual cues later than experts. Perceptual training can enhance the ability to pick up subtle visual and other cues earlier in the viewing process, such as an opponent's contact point, posture, balance, and footwork. Focus on the ball as early as possible and become attuned to spin, height, direction, pace, and location. Experienced players do this; more experience develops greater attunement to visual cues, such as an opponent's posture, balance, and position on the court. Expert tennis players are more effective and efficient in their visual search behaviors because they've learned where to look and they possess greater knowledge of situational probabilities. Expert players are also more attuned to other senses such as hearing the ball off their opponent's racket and feeling the ball off their racket, as well as feeling other events, such as wind. Hearing provides information regarding spin and how hard the ball is hit. Feeling wind provides information, allowing anticipation as to how the ball will travel through the air. Training specific to the cues can improve perception and, consequently, reaction by expediting and enhancing visual and sensory attunement.

To demonstrate the difference between novice, recreational, and expert players, Coach Wayne Elderton uses a concept called focus of attention range (FAR). Elderton's FAR concept is actually a way of looking at perception. Players of differing abilities in terms of visual acuity may "see" something at about the same time, but better players "perceive" the event sooner, in that their brains interpret visual signals more quickly to proceed to act. Where a player "perceives" the ball is his focus of attention range (FAR).

For instance, beginners have a FAR that starts about the service line on their side of the court. They see the approaching ball immediately from where the opponent hits it; however, nothing registers until the ball is about to bounce, and then they react. Of course, this is a generalization, and players who are good athletes and have successfully played other sports may have a more developed FAR.

Intermediate players have a FAR that starts around the net. It is like the ball they see is in a fog. When the ball comes out of the fog, it registers with them to react.

Advanced players have a FAR that includes the opponent on the far end of the court. They pick up relevant clues right from the opponent's impact of the ball.

An elite player has a FAR that encompasses the opponent and also includes gathering clues to anticipate the characteristics of the opponent's shot.

So, what cues should one look to to enhance performance? Look to your opponent. See what he is doing. More specifically, look to your opponent's hitting forearm and racket, because that is where the ball will come from. Simply, and even more specifically, learn to look to the ball coming off your opponent's racket.

In the martial arts, one goes from soft focus to hard focus. With the initial encounter, the fighter perceives the general situation, checking his opponent's stance, balance, leg and arm positions, along with the overall surroundings. This is the soft focus that in essence perceives the entire general situation.

Then as the action begins, one turns his focus to the specific point of attack, looking to and anticipating the greatest threat.

This is the hard focus, which is almost tunnel vision or peephole concentration.

Soft focus is general. Hard focus is specific.

Try practicing what tennis student Laura Martin calls the yup drill, a drill intended to enhance earlier perception. Try identifying when the ball is on your opponent's racket and call out "Yup" or "Hit." Do the same when the ball bounces on your side of the court, calling out "Yup" or "Bounce." This helps heighten awareness of the ball as it relates to your opponent as he hits and as it relates to you when the ball is on your side of the court.

In developing perceptual skills, learn to go from soft to hard focus. In tennis, the point of greatest threat generally comes from your opponent's racket. Learn to focus on your opponent's racket and the ball coming off the racket. Train yourself to go from soft focus before your opponent's impact to hard focus at impact. Train yourself to "see" and "perceive" the ball coming off your opponent's racket as well as when it bounces on your side of the court to when you make contact. Learn to develop that "peephole" concentration that focuses on one thing.

In baseball, Robson discusses relaxing the eyes and looking from big to little, eventually leading to the pitcher's arm slot. This is another way of articulating hard focus or the peephole concentration needed for "this pitch, this moment." In tennis, rather than looking at the baseball pitcher's arm slot, instead look to the opponent's racket and ball.

According to baseball coach Paul Reddick,

> Ted Williams said "get a good pitch to hit." Notice he didn't say swing at a good pitch or hit a good pitch, he said "get a good pitch."

The pitch breaks up into two parts.

Part 1: Everything from the time a pitcher starts his windup to halfway point of the pitch. That is the "get," the getting a good pitch to hit. The first half of the pitch is when a hitter is going to read the pitch, take his stride and decide whether he's going to swing or not swing.

Part 2: Continue to swing or hold up.

What the batter does in that first half of the pitch determines what happens the rest of the way. (P. Reddick, personal communication December 1, 2016)

Part 1 is perception, pure and simple, while part 2 is reaction. Reddick notes baseball coaches generally deal primarily with the action/reaction phase without focusing on the essential initial perception phase, to the hitter's detriment.

At this point, in tennis and any sport coupling perception with reaction, you need to react. However, your job of anticipation and perception is not done. In fact, it is never done. Continually throughout the shot process in tennis, you adapt and change your anticipation as you change your perception. Even as you react, you continue to perceive, anticipate, and adjust as you move, as you track the ball, and as you set up and stroke the ball.

To help with your vision and perception throughout the moving and stroking process, keep your head balanced and still. Keeping your head still affects not only your balance, but also the way you actually see! By keeping your head still, you can stabilize your eyes to maintain a steady gaze pattern. As you move, you still need to maximize your ability to see and perceive. If your head is bouncing around, your eyes are also bouncing. Bouncing eyes are unfocused eyes. To maximize vision and perception, keep your head as still as possible, which in turn allows you to see and perceive with more focus.

Later on in the point sequence, you will need again to assume hard focus as you set up and stroke the ball. This time your hard focus is on the ball as it bounces on your side, tracking it to your racket's contact point. Again, the more still your head is, the better you can see and focus hard.

Maintaining a stable gaze is important, and a stable head allows for a stable gaze. Robson notes the hitter needs to keep his head and eyes parallel to the ground so that he can recognize the pitch correctly. When the head is stable, that is to say strong and still, the hitter has his best chance of recognizing the pitch.

Reaction

Always Split Step

Reaction is how the brain, upon perceiving, sends the signals to and activates the body to move. How do you improve your reaction? Well, to begin with, be ready to react! What does this mean? In tennis, always split step.

No matter what shot you're hitting (except for the serve), always get ready to react and move by split stepping on the balls of your feet. Wherever you are, whether in the proverbial "no man's land" or not, no matter what the situation, *always* split step when your opponent makes contact with the ball. The split step is like the starting blocks for a track sprinter; it allows you the position to thrust forward to the next shot. The split step makes you quicker, both in reacting and in moving.

Earlier, as a drill to develop and enhance perception, we suggested the "yup" drill, where the player calls out "yup" when the opponent hits the ball and also when the ball bounces on the player's side of the court. To help with reaction and improving one's perception/reaction coupling, work to split step by the time the opponent hits the ball, and then work to set up by the time the ball hits the court on your side.

Another simple training drill is using a reaction ball, an unevenly sided rubber ball that bounces unpredictably when dropped. Using a reaction ball almost mandates hard focus and split stepping if one is to consistently catch the ball after one bounce.

Subliminal Reaction and Action: Developing Flow

We've talked about anticipation, seeing, perception, and reaction, which all is quite a bit. However, we're not done. Additionally, the improving athlete who wants to attain mastery needs to make this whole process automatic and unconscious in a way in which everything flows.

For novices or inexperienced athletes in a sport such as a martial arts, tennis, or baseball, the connection or coupling from anticipation to perception to reaction/action is slowed by conscious processing. Repetitions, practice, and experience help narrow, expedite, or even change this processing to move action from conscious, explicit action to automatic, implicit, almost subconscious action.

One of the keys in mastery of any physical activity involving action and reaction is to achieve implicit, subliminal, almost automatic, flowing performance. Some call this accommodation; others such as Matthew Syed, in *Bounce: The Myth of Talent and the Power of Practice*, refers to this as implicit action. Tim Gallwey, in *The Inner Game of Tennis*, calls this "playing out of your mind." Steven Yellin, in *The 7 Secrets of World Class Athletes*, refers to this as the fluid motion factor, which removes the perception/action coupling from the prefrontal cortex to the brain's motor system. Closely related is the flow inherent in ying and yang.

How does subliminal action occur? Yellin believes that conscious, critical intellectual action occurs in the brain's prefrontal cortex, while fluid motion takes place in the brain's motor system. The prefrontal cortex's intellectual conscious thinking slows reaction and fluid motion. By commanding the body to try hard, it may actually impede speed, power, flow, and performance by tightening and shortening the muscles. The key is to condition performance to minimize the prefrontal cortex and maximize action within the brain's automatic motor system.

One of the key differences between a novice and an experienced performer is that the novice necessarily has to consciously figure out what he is doing while the experienced athlete acts and reacts automatically. The novice perceives something and then almost consciously thinks, "Now, what do I do?" The expert perceives something and acts or reacts immediately.

Yellin believes that perception/reaction signals that immediately go to the motor system result in fluid, effortless, effective, and faster motion. But an interfering prefrontal cortex necessarily slows reaction, resulting in less fluid, effortless, and effective motion. The key is to eliminate the prefrontal cortex's involvement so that directives for movement and execution come from the motor system. World-class athletes, according to Yellin, are able to keep the prefrontal cortex from interfering with signals moving to the motor system and thus allow Yellin's so-called fluid motion factor to occur. Gallwey calls this "Self 2," which inheres a staggering inner intelligence, utilizing billions of cells and neurological communication circuits in every action.

In his incisively entertaining article on Roger Federer "Federer Both Flesh and Not," contained in *String Theory*, essayist and former competitive junior player David Foster Wallace notes that "the upshot is that pro tennis involves intervals of time too brief for deliberate action. Temporally, we're more in the operative range of reflexes, purely physical reactions that bypass conscious thought."

A common example of initial explicit learning that develops into implicit action occurs with learning to drive a car. When first learning to drive, everything seems foreign and detached. We learn that the car goes when we step on the accelerator and slows or stops when we push the brake pedal. Initially we are separate from the seeming behemoth of a machine car, and driving is a supremely conscious journey. Feeling the car move when we step on the pedal is an adventure fraught with potential danger, and braking often results in a comedy of herky-jerky, quick stops and gos.

However, as we learn and as we drive more and more, the act of driving becomes second nature, to the point that accelerating and braking become automatic implicit actions and reactions, depending on the circumstances. Driving is a quintessential example of the marriage and automatic blending between anticipation, vision, perception, and reaction. Experienced drivers implicitly drive with flow. The formerly explicit conscious act has morphed into automatic subliminal blending of the driver with the car. In reality, the driver has extended himself into and through the car. Mastery and true learning in sports and activity require this kind of morphing or blending so that movement, action, and reaction become automatic, whether in fighting, tennis, or other sports.

How do we attain implicit, subliminal action and reaction? Practice, practice, and more practice. Repetition, repetition, and more repetition. Keep working and practicing until your movement, action, and reaction become automatic.

David Foster Wallace notes the double benefit, muscular and neurological, that practice and constant repetitions provide an individual. "Hitting thousands of strokes, day after day, develops the ability to do by 'feel' what cannot be done by regular conscious thought. Repetitive practice like this often looks tedious or even cruel to an outsider, but the outsider can't feel what's going on inside the player—tiny adjustments, over and over, and a sense of each change's effects that gets more and more acute even as it recedes from normal consciousness."

These repetitions apply throughout tennis. Advanced players are often advanced because they are more experienced; they have simply hit more balls, played more matches, and have spent more time on the court to allow for faster processing of anticipatory and perceptual information, which in turn increases the changes to develop subliminal flow.

So, understanding the need to develop anticipation, perception, and reaction, how does one improve? Is this simply an academic exercise so that one intellectually understands why experts are expert while novices are novices, or are there ways to improve? Good news! If you want to improve, you can. To review and to improve in each area of the anticipation, visual, perception, reaction, and subliminal action connection trail, practice the following:

- Anticipation—readiness for the greatest threat; know and watch your opponent; note the speed, spin, height, and direction of your opponent's ball; know what your opponent likes to do under pressure.
- Vision—get your eyes checked by an optometrist or ophthalmologist.
- Perception—practice the yup drill; go from soft to hard focus, keying on your opponent's forearm and racket and the ball off his racket.

- Reaction—always split step; practice with a reaction ball.
- Subliminal automatic action/reaction—practice, practice, practice.

Elsewhere in this book we talk about the kinetic chain and the need for energy to flow from the ground through the body eventually into the racket and ball. A break in the kinetic chain breaks energy flow, limiting one's momentum and force. Similarly, the perceptual chain runs from anticipation to sight to perception to reaction. A weakness in any of these links weakens the perceptual/reaction chain, hindering performance.

Remember:
The fact is that one cannot perform well in self-defense or fast-action sports as baseball and tennis without anticipating, seeing, perceiving, and reacting.
The better you anticipate, the better you see and perceive.
The better you see, the better you perceive.
The better you perceive, the better you react.
The better you react, the better you perform.
Furthermore, the more automatic you make this whole process, the closer you come to mastery.

CHAPTER ELEVEN

MOVEMENT, SETUP, AND BALANCE

Many preach the necessity for balance, but few actually focus on balance. What is balance? The *Compact Oxford English Dictionary* defines *balance* as "a state in which weight is distributed equally, enabling a person or thing to remain steady and upright." In martial arts, tennis, and other athletics, one must master both static balance and dynamic balance. Static balance is balance when one is steady and upright while still. Dynamic balance is balance when one is steady and upright while moving.

Ease of movement and footwork is essential to a proper balanced setup. When moving, move from your center, the ki point just below your navel and between the hips. Most novices move from the upper body or shoulders, coming off-balance. Move from the center.

Improper balance prevents you from moving quickly and effectively. Your optimal balance point is your ki point. Keep your balance point at your ki by distributing your weight equally over your hips and by properly positioning your feet. Always keep your feet moving to maintain your center of gravity near your navel where it belongs.

The ki point is essential for moving, defending, and striking; and it applies to other sports and physical activities as well as martial arts. Moving from the center is consistently fundamental throughout sports, whether it is baseball, basketball, surfing, soccer, even surfing, fencing, and dancing. Definitely, the need to move from the center and to maintain balance from the ki is fundamental for tennis too.

In discussing balance, Koga notes that one of the most common faults in self-defense is the failure to move the entire body. The biggest hazard lies in upper body movements without compensating foot, leg, and hip movements. Use the hips, legs, and feet to maintain a balanced center of gravity.

Kiegiel notes the outstanding characteristic of the expert athlete is his or her ease of movement, epitomizing ying and yang. Fluid movement comes only if a relaxed state of ying yields in a smooth transition to the forceful motions of yang.

Koga tells police officers not to reach out from a position of interrogation to grab at a subject. If they do, they'll find themselves precariously off-balance. Rather, they should move the whole body, keeping the center of gravity between the navel and the hips, and they should *always, always* keep their balance.

In baseball, Robson acknowledges the utility of the center point. In his book he asks one to think of the belly button as the center or core of the body. Robson notes that by controlling his center of gravity, a hitter can focus his entire body on performing a certain task.

When off-balance, you tend to tighten up as your body fights gravity's effects. Tightening creates tension; tension destroys power. Intuitively, your mind senses when you are off-balance or falling, and you tend to rush technique in an almost momentary panic mode. When off-balance, you lose the ability to rotate effectively, thus impairing power in another way. When off-balance, you cannot use your legs and lower body effectively: instead, you rely on your arms and hands. Using the arms and hands rather than the bigger muscles of the legs and hips means using less mass with more variables, thus reducing power and consistency and dramatically increasing the chances of failure.

In *Night Stick*, martial arts author Joseph Hess says, "The key to gaining control is balance and leverage. Pay special attention to stances and footwork. If you rely solely on upper body power to execute these techniques, they will not work properly." Robert Koga echoes this in *Police Weaponless Control and Defense Techniques*.

A proper balanced setup comes via good posture and a balanced body alignment rising from the ground through the legs, hips, core, upper torso, head, arms, and hands. The balanced setup *is basically the same* for almost all sports. What does this mean?

> Keep the knees over the balls of your feet.
> Keep your armpits over your knees.
> Keep your back straight.
> Keep your shoulders level.
> Keep your head still and stable on top.

Why are balance and setup important? Because power flows from the ground up. Ground force translates to the setup in two words: *posture* and *balance*. Basic to martial arts, the ground is the power source literally at your feet. With a balanced setup, ground force allows you to move from your setup ying to your stroke's yang, allowing you to turn loose your stroke with an incredible power surge from the ground up. You can only do this if your feet are comfortably rooted and balanced.

A proper setup allows one to maximize power from the ground by utilizing the kinetic chain through the body forward into the target. Execute techniques first from the body with the arms following. Many ignore the critical setup, focusing primarily on the arms, to their detriment. Stay strong and aggressive with the legs and lower body, with the arms following almost passively.

TENNIS

Tennis is all about moving and setting up with balance. Make your goal to be on balance for every shot (and to get your opponent off-balance). Most mistakes come from not setting up in time and on balance. Work hard to set up, then let go and flow with the stroke. Set up. Let go.

When balanced, you use the mass of your body rather than just your arms. Using your body's mass provides more stability, more power, and more control. Power, rhythm, and control—that is to say everything comes from balance. A tip: keep your chin up. Keeping your chin up will help maintain stability and balance; keeping your chin up minimizes the chance that you will lower your head, bend at the waist, and lose your balance.

Keep your arms and hands in front of your sternum. Another way of looking at this is to always keep your elbows in front of your body. When moving, move your body rather than your arms. Move as if someone is pulling you with a rope tied around your waist, not as if it is tied around your head or neck. Keep moving from the center, no matter what stroke you're hitting.

Setting up involves getting the racket in position, as well as the body. Use the body to get the racket in position; don't wrist the ball. If you are moving your feet, you won't have to move your hands. If you are moving your hands, you're probably not moving your feet!

Wherever you go on the court, keep your balance. When moving forward to the net, it is better to stop early rather than late, because stopping early allows you to maintain balance; stopping late takes you off-balance.

When you move to stroke a tennis ball, imagine that you are moving to catch the ball. The goal is to move to catch, not to hit. Keep in mind your motive. Maintain your motive to catch. By maintaining your motive to catch (rather than hit), you keep your arms, elbows, and hands in front of your body, thus allowing you to stay balanced, utilizing your body mass and achieving a better contact point through the actual stroke.

Three Keys to Footwork

Footwork! What is it? Is it moving your feet real fast? Bouncing on your toes twenty times between shots? It is very hard to work on something you have not defined. The three keys to footwork are as follows:

1. Set up as if you're hitting down the line.
2. Set up as if you're going to net, with your energy flowing forward.
3. Hit (catch) the ball in the power zone, between your knees and shoulders.

Setting up as if you're going down the line makes you work to move your feet to get in position really to hit anywhere in the court. Setting up as if you're going down the line makes you move more, load more aggressively, and get your body mass behind the ball better.

By setting up as if you're going down the line, you actually have the option of going down the line. If you want to go crosscourt, still set up as if you're going down the line, but simply release the racket into the ball a bit earlier. Always setting up to go down the line is easier said than done. The key, as always, is with the feet. To set up down the line requires aggressive and energetic footwork.

Setting up as if you're going to net makes you work to get behind the ball so that you move your body mass into the ball, thus providing better balance, power, and control. Always set up as if you're going to net with your energy flowing forward into the ball. By setting up in this fashion, you are better balanced, more controlled, more powerful, and have more options.

Stroking the ball between your knees and shoulders makes you work so that you stroke the ball in your comfort/power zone, thus increasing the chances for more consistent play, more balanced play, and more powerful play.

If you don't set up and maintain balance, mistakes inevitably occur. Off-balance play is mistake-riddled play.

Watch the world's top professionals play. See how they move. Watch their feet. Just by observing a professional player's feet, you can tell whether he will make the shot or miss. When balanced behind the ball, the world's top professionals don't miss. Errors only creep in when they are not balanced and not behind the ball.

We all can learn much from this. Work hard to move to get balanced and behind the ball, and you will stroke better with fewer errors. In short, work hard to move to get balanced and set up behind the ball, and you will improve.

Split Step and Leverage

Obviously, the first link between the ground and your body is your feet; the feet connect the body to the ground. It is here where one has the first opportunity to leverage one's body with the ground, to use ground force to drive off and move quickly.

Earlier in chapter 10 we talked about the split step as fundamentally important in anticipating and reacting. The split step is also essential in providing quick and effective leverage of the feet with the ground, allowing for a strong push off.

Some experts talk about the "drop step." The so-called drop step is the reactionary step where one steps slightly to the outside to drive off the ground in the opposite direction. Rather than think of drop stepping, we like to think of split stepping aggressively with a wider base so that one can react and drive to the ball or oncoming shot much as a sprinter reacts and drives out of the starting blocks in a race.[4] Often tennis players and other athletes will split step with a narrower base and thus have to take an additional small drop step to react and get going. The more effective approach is to split step with a wider base, thus lowering the body and further engaging the legs, so that one can immediately react and drive off the split step in the direction of the oncoming ball.

Feel your feet on the ground. Feel how your feet interact with the ground. Many athletes are not aware of their feet and their connection to the ground. Develop your kinesthetic sense, your proprioception, your feel of your feet connecting to the ground and your body. Develop your sense and you'll start to maximize your leverage of your feet with essential ground force, making yourself quicker and stronger.

Your feet provide contact and leverage with the ground. This applies not only to starting and moving but also to stopping, an integral part of setting up. As you develop your sense of feet connecting with the ground, feel the connection with stopping

---

[4] Watch what happens when a track sprinter drives out of the starting blocks. The sprinter actually appears to drive the upper body out of the blocks so much that he almost falls. Then, while almost falling, the sprinter pulls his hips underneath his body to regain balance, a move that produces efficient acceleration. The same dynamic results in tennis when driving from a wide base off the split step.

as well as starting. Learn to get your planting foot to the outside or behind where the ball is coming so that you can set up with strength and balance. As with the initial split step to react and drive, feel the planting foot on the ground as it plants and drives into the oncoming ball.

The Rhythm of Setting Up

Earlier we talked about anticipation and readiness for the fastball. Training for the fastball necessarily involves greater alertness and more intense readiness to react to the ball off your opponent's racket. Sometimes this preliminary intensity leads to more relaxed stroking. Tennis is such a game of paradoxes, and readying yourself for the greatest threat presents another one. By focusing on and being ready for the fastball, one engages sooner in moving and preparing for the shot, to the extent that he often gets to the ball sooner, sets up sooner with more balance, and then hits a smoother, more relaxed shot.

Roger Federer is one of the masters and a great example of this. People tend to remember Federer as a smooth, effortless shot maker, seemingly always in position, and almost never rushed. This perception often comes from the way spectators watch tennis. Usually they watch the player stroking the ball. Once one person hits the ball, spectators usually shift their attention to the person on the other side of the net to see how he strokes the ball. What happens for spectators is a constant shifting of attention from player to another, focusing on the time each hits the ball.

What they tend not to see is what the other player does in between shots. So, for most spectators, their memories of Roger Federer is that he almost always seems to be waiting for the ball come to him, and then set up, relaxed and with balance, effortlessly stroking the ball back. For them, Roger makes the game look easy. What spectators tend not to see is the work and sheer effort Roger does to move *between shots.* Federer's effort and intensity between shots are remarkable, allowing him to get in position and stroke as if the game is easy.

Emulate Roger Federer. Get into the rhythm of setting up and stroking. Try mantras like the following with your movement and setup:

"Work, work, work . . . relax."
or
"Move, move, move . . . relax."

Most players do not utilize this rhythm of setting up. Perhaps many find a different rhythm more familiar, such as this:
"Relax, relax, oh my goodness! The ball is coming fast, panic, HIT!"

Does this seem familiar? Most people tend to take the time afforded to them to practice inertia and wait until the last possible moment to move. This is *not* a recipe for success. Break out of that habit, and get into the rhythm of setting up for the fastball, irrespective whether the fastball exists. "Work hard to get ready, then relax" is much, much better than "Relax and then panic hard to get ready." Get into a mantra such as this:

"Move, move, move . . . relax."

Now, you've got into the rhythm mantra. You've moved and worked hard to set up, and you've now got time to relax and hit your target.

Try to Set Up by the Time the Ball Bounces

To work on setting up, try moving to set up and balance by the time the ball bounces on your side of the court. While some do this fairly naturally, most do not. Focusing on this helps you set up more quickly and more effectively. Of course, you can't set up this way on every shot; however, see how many balls you can fully set up by the time they bounce. By doing this, you gain a better knowledge and understanding of whether you are ready to hit your shot. Simply increasing your awareness of whether you are set up also helps in your shot selection, whether to hit offensively, neutrally, or defensively.

After Each Shot, Appear as if You're Going Forward to Net

Look like you are going to the net after every shot. If you watch Rafael Nadal, even when the ball is hit in the middle of the court, he runs around and looks as if he is going inside out on his forehand. Novak Djokovic always appears to set up as if going forward and down the line. His energy and mass move forward as he hits the ball in his power zone, between his knees and shoulders. Learn from these champions. When moving forward on any stroke, do so with your legs and hips, not with your head. Keep your head over your hips, always (if you can).

OTHER SPORTS

Balance and equilibrium are the same everywhere, whether in the weight room lifting weights, on the martial arts mat, on the golf course, on the baseball diamond, or on the tennis court. Keep a solid base with your body well anchored to the ground. Without balance and stability, techniques are ineffective.

It is widely believed that tennis greats John McEnroe and Rafael Nadal could have played high-level soccer. Why? In watching them play tennis, both McEnroe and Nadal keep a wide base and balance. Those abilities transfer from sport to sport, and it is not surprising that they could also probably succeed with soccer.

Robson notes in baseball that the hitter must maintain balance and train the body to work in sequence. As mentioned, dynamic balance utilizes strong posture to control the center of gravity from start to finish. To stabilize the body, keep the head over the belly button and keep the base wide.

In golf, controlling ground forces is achieved through balance. Again, every sport requires balance and equilibrium. Tennis is no different.

Kiegiel notes that most golfers underestimate the importance of their setup. Without a proper setup, no one swings properly. For golf he recommends the following:

Front View
- Shoulders and hips level
- Eyes parallel to the ground
- Head vertical and neck ninety degrees to shoulders
- Shoulders over hips
- Hips over knees

Side View
- Ears over shoulders
- Shoulders over hips
- Hips over knees
- Knees over ankles

In checking out the setup for golf, the same balanced alignment also can easily apply to tennis, baseball, or even the defensive position in basketball. In evaluating one's balance, note how often these positions are *not* observed. Simply working on one's balance and attaining a proper alignment will immediately enhance performance.

Earlier, in discussing tennis, we said that one should always set up as if to hit down the line. Top volleyball coach Jeff Hall says the same thing about setting up to hit a volleyball. By setting up to hit down the line, the volleyball striker is better balanced with more options, including hitting down the line, through the middle, or crosscourt. Furthermore, the hitter gets her body better through the shot while more effectively disguising the shot. The reasons for setting up as if to hit down the line apply equally whether the sport is volleyball or tennis.

Remember:
Stay balanced always.
Balance—everyone talks about it; not everyone feels it.
Without balance, you lose power, rhythm, and composure.
Without balance, urgency and panic rule your mind.
Without balance, you will want to rush
your stroke before you fall.
Without balance, as you feel your body fall, you
automatically lift, losing power, rhythm, and composure.
Stay balanced for power, rhythm, and composure.

CHAPTER TWELVE

GROUND FORCE AND THE KINETIC CHAIN

The martial arts, as Kiegiel notes, teach that nature has engineered the human body for fluid and effective movement. Only if we obey the natural law of body alignment do we tap our bodies' full balance and power. Correct body alignment creates maximum balance and power from minimal effort. Conversely, the natural law provides that if any key area is misaligned, the other parts can't work as well. Natural law supplies maximum balance and power from an aligned and relaxed state.

What are the key areas?

- Legs and hips
- Ki/core
- Upper torso and shoulders
- Head
- Arms and hands

Power comes from the ground. Utilize your body's kinetic chain to hit from the ground, tapping into earth's essential power. Keep your upper body and lower torso stable with your shoulders level. Keep your head still. Move aggressively with the legs and lower body, keeping the upper body and arms relatively passive. Lower with the legs. Turn the hips and let the rest follow.

Legs and Hips

In martial arts, the back leg is the power and balance leg. The same rings true in hitting a baseball; the hitter transfers force from the back foot to the front foot when moving to make contact. The sequence is similar in golf, tennis, and practically in all sports.

In martial arts, turn the hips to pull your adversary off-balance. Often the untrained person will try to outmuscle his opponent by using his arms and hands. Using the arms usually will pull the puller off-balance, compromising his position. The body's power lies in the legs and hips, rather than the arms. Stay aggressive with the legs and hips while relaxed elsewhere, including the arms and hands.

A hitter doesn't bend over to hit a low pitch or to bunt. Instead, he lowers his body with his legs and keeps his head somewhat over his center of gravity. Many athletes in many sports incorrectly bend from the waist to get lower, breaking the kinetic chain and losing essential ground force. In any sport, when crouching, go straight down by lowering the legs, not by bending at the waist.

For instance, in baseball bunting, Robson says pitches down in the strike zone must be bunted from squatting with the legs, not by bending at the waist. On a low pitch, many bunters make the mistake of bending over, changing the relationship of the eyes and bat to the pitch, making it more difficult to see and successfully bunt. Bending also takes one off-balance, impairing stability and breaking the all-important kinetic chain.

In golf, Malaska sees that the hip girdle is one of the major power sources in the swing. If the hips over-rotate at impact, one taps only a portion of one's true power output. The body creates power and speed through rotation. The turning motion of the hip girdle is a natural process. Just let it happen.

The same rings true for boxing. Author F. X. Toole, in *Million Dollar Baby*, uses character Frankie Dunn to explain to fighter Maggie Fitzgerald:

First, you go to line up at a forty-five degree angle, understand? And then you got to turn your waist as you punch. When you throw a right-hand, you got to step out to the left six inches as you move half a step in with both feet. That frees your right hip and leg and foot, like this, so you can *snap* your ass into your shots.

The tendency of most is to release the hips too soon, whether in golf, baseball, or tennis. One's job is to store power so that it releases fully at impact. Release too soon and you've prematurely unloaded. While this is a matter of timing, perhaps more relevant for advanced players, players can benefit from waiting just a split second longer before unloading the hips so as to more effectively harness the kinetic energy from the ground through the hips. The bottom line is that if you delay the rotation of your hip girdle until the moment of impact, you will hit the ball cleaner, longer, and straighter in golf, further in baseball, and with more power and spin in tennis.

Ki/Core

As mentioned before, some refer to the ki one point as an actual place in the body, slightly below the navel. Most keep their athletic balance higher than their ki one point. Simply by lowering your core athletic center of gravity to your ki one point, you'll improve stability, balance, and performance.

Upper Torso and Shoulders

Where your shoulders go, your arms follow. Trust the kinetic chain. So many athletes mistakenly rely on their arms and hands for power, ignoring ground force and the kinetic chain. The shoulders are an integral part of the kinetic chain as energy flows from the ground through the body into the shoulders and into the arms and hands. Furthermore, when you turn your shoulders, naturally your arms go along for the ride. Use your shoulders to maximize your kinetic chain.

Play tennis in front of your body. Turn your body to get the racket in position. By doing this, tennis actually becomes more of a lower-body sport. Turn your body to keep your arms and hands in front of your sternum. When moving, move your sternum rather than your arms.

Head

Keep the head still and balanced on top of your shoulders.

Just as with the importance of footwork, one cannot overemphasize the need for a still and quiet head. The head weighs a lot, more than most think. Moving the head almost certainly pulls you off-balance. Keep your head still and you'll simplify your balance.

In baseball, a successful hitter keeps his head still. Robson says that if the batter moves his head to track the ball, "he is defying one of the absolutes that allows the body to create force during motion—one body part cannot accelerate forward until another body part stops." Keep your body posture strong. Keep your eyes level and still. Your body will rotate better if you keep your head still. The more stabilized the head, the faster the body rotates sequentially.

The need for a still and balanced head applies throughout sport. Keeping one's head still is axiomatic in golf. Because the head is relatively heavy, just moving it a bit changes one's balance. Whatever you do for sport, keep your head still and on top of your shoulders.

Here's a tip to help keep the head balanced and on top of your shoulders. Keep your chin up. Many tend to drop the chin just a bit, thus pulling their head down. While it may seem like a small thing, keeping the chin up provides greater alignment, balance, and leverage. Keeping the chin up allows the body to work surprisingly easier and more effectively.

Arms and Hands

To maintain connectedness and a strong position, keep the arms, elbows, and hands in front of the body. Keeping in mind the principle that good techniques flow from the ground up, keeping the arms and hands in front, keep balance and connection with the ground. Bringing the arms back or off to the side of one's body takes one off-balance, losing ground connectivity.

In stick fighting, you'll see combatants swinging sticks faster and faster, building up amazing kinetic energy, the type of energy that can defend, disable, and maim. To the untrained observer, the stick looks as if it is out of control, but in reality, the combatant controls his stick by controlling his body and feeling the weapon with his fingers. By doing so with a loose grip, the weapon becomes an extension of his body.

Most athletes who use a stick, bat, club, or racket grip too tightly. A tight grip impedes power. Relax and loosen the fingers to let the ground force move through the hands into your weapon, bat, club, or racket. Let the body's energy flow from the ground through the body, into the arm, hand, and fingers. Natural law governs all physical movement, whether in golf, baseball, martial arts, tennis, or any other athletic motion.

Biomechanically, the position of your hand when shaking hands is the strongest position. Has anyone in tennis ever said this? Perhaps some have, but the pronouncement is not common.

However, martial artists have known this for thousands of years. A tennis player might think that tennis is different from martial arts. While it is different, tennis is merely a sport, while martial arts developed as disciplines of defense and survival. Martial arts principles ring true as they have survived, almost literally, through the ages.

In an older time, in a prior generation, many of us were taught to volley with the racket head above the handle. In many situations, this command still rings true, particularly with balls above waist level. Yet John McEnroe arrived on the scene and showed the world how to volley on lower balls with the racket head below the handle. How did he do this? By keeping a biomechanically strong handshake position between the hand and wrist (and by keeping his contact point in front of his body).

At the moment of impact, whether on ground strokes or volleys, the handshake position is the hand position you want. Work on getting that position at impact and, on ground strokes, simply follow through the ball with your wrist and racket.

The martial arts stick fighter feels the weapon with his fingers, making the weapon an extension of his body. The same applies to tennis. Keep your balance and a loose grip, and your racket becomes an extension of you, subject to your control. Feel the racket as part of your body and stroke with your fingers.

Stroking with your fingers requires a loose grip. Relax your hands and fingers. Let your body's energy flow from the ground through your body into your arm, hand, and fingers.

Almost all tennis players grip their racket much too tightly. On a relative scale from 1 to 10, with 1 as the loosest grip and 10 the tightest, try for a 3 level tightness grip. Most players report a normal grip of a 5, 6, or 7. Loosening to a 3 level allows for better feel and more acceleration. A looser grip allows the racket to do its work. Conversely, a tighter grip inhibits acceleration, power, and racket-head speed.

In *The Inner Game of Tennis*, Gallwey quotes Cyrano de Bergerac in learning to fence: "Hold the foil as a bird, not so loosely that it can fly away, but not so tightly that you squeeze the life out of it."

The release of the tennis racket in the serve is almost identical to the golf swing release. The power of the serve is dependent on the relaxation of the wrists and its ability to release when you hit. In golf, Malaska notes that the more relaxed the wrists, the quicker the club can move through impact.

Sometimes coaches talk about snapping the bat in baseball, snapping the golf club into the ball, or snapping the tennis racket into the serve. We prefer the term *release* instead of *snap*. Feeling the release (rather than a snap) allows for more flow, consistent with ying and yang. Releasing, rather than snapping, provides a subliminal positive reaction, allowing and utilizing the kinetic chain to provide more torque and leverage. Releasing provides a flow so that when one side stops, the other accelerates.

In golf, Malaska also notes that perfecting the grip allows one to access the greatest amount of power from the body and swing, putting this energy into the club and ball. Keep the fingers loose. Tight hands and fingers create unnecessary tension, tension that impedes timing and rhythm. Additionally, tight fingers and hands can cause the rest of the body to tighten, right up through the upper torso.

The body moves to assist and accommodate the arm swing, whether in golf, tennis, baseball, or other sports. The arms and hands control the tennis racket, golf club, or baseball bat. Power comes from the ground through the legs, hips and upper torso. By the time that kinetic energy reaches the hands, racket, and ball, if done properly, a lot of power and force is in play. By that time in the stroke, centrifugal force has taken over and the hands are along for the ride. Tightening the hands simply breaks the kinetic chain. Keep the hands loose, let them go for the ride, and let the force awaken.

Beginners especially and even many advanced players play tennis with the hand and arm first and the body second. This makes sense intuitively for someone picking up a racket and stepping on the court for the very first time. The beginner who has never stroked a tennis ball will think simply and act along the following lines:

> I have a racket in my hand. There is a ball, and I must use the racket to hit the ball over the net. Because the racket is in my hand, I must use my hand. Because I must use my hand to hold the racket to hit the ball over the net, I must focus on my hand and arm.

This approach is perfectly understandable and makes common sense, superficially. However, this beginning common sense approach ignores the essential ground force, the kinetic chain, the legs, and the hips.

The dog wags the tail.
The elephant swings his trunk.

Truly, the tail does not wag the dog. The trunk does not swing the elephant. Likewise in tennis, the legs and hips swing the arms and hands; the arms and hands cannot control the body.

Additionally, by focusing on and moving the arm and hand first in stroking, the arm's natural motion takes over the stroke, creating instability and more room for error. In swinging the arm first, the outside ulna bone naturally rotates the wrist over the inside radius bone. The arm's natural swing rotating the ulna over the radius necessarily rotates the racket face during the swing and increases the chances for error. By stroking first with the arm, the margin for error increases, making solid contact more difficult.

Instead of swinging with the arm first, let the legs and hips do their work, with the arm, hand, and racket going along for the ride, and then releasing. By letting the legs and hips do the initial work of rotating, the arm, notably the ulna and radius bones, remains stable. A stable arm allows for a stable racket face as the legs and hips rotate through the ball. Only upon contact do the arm and wrist release the racket through the ball and follow through. This is all part of putting it all together, essential for striking, which we talk about next.

Remember:
Your hands and arms tighten when you
don't feel power from the ground.
Stay connected to the ground.
Keep your arms and hands relaxed
as you feel the ground force
through your body.

CHAPTER THIRTEEN

PUTTING IT ALL TOGETHER: ROTATION AND STRIKING

Martial arts may seem mystical and exotic, but nature's laws of physics apply everywhere, including when striking. People are mystified by the power that martial arts produce, but really and simply, the laws of physics apply. Applied physics dictate that force equals mass times acceleration. No matter what the activity, whether martial arts, tennis, or any other sport, use the larger muscle groups and ground force to increase striking mass while utilizing the kinetic chain to accelerate.

Force = Mass × Acceleration

The *faster* something moves, the more force it generates. Also, the more *mass* something has, the more force it can generate. To generate maximum force, you must increase mass and speed together.

Therefore, in tennis, a heavier racket has greater potential for power, provided the player can accelerate it quickly. Similarly, using the body's larger muscle groups to stroke the ball, such as the legs and hips, utilizes greater mass and thus generates greater power. Use the body to stroke the ball and you'll generate more force and a heavier ball.

Additionally, learn to accelerate the larger muscle groups in sequence with your arms and hands, and you'll generate tremendous force. Accelerate quickly with the greatest mass you can, and good things happen.

Momentum

Momentum is the force gained by a moving object. There are two types of momentum: linear and angular. Linear momentum is energy created by driving and accelerating in a straight line. Angular momentum is energy created from rotational force.

Almost all tennis shots involve a blend or combination of angular and linear momentum. However, angular momentum generally generates more acceleration through rotation and, therefore, more force. While linear and angular momentum each produce acceleration, angular momentum generates more through rotation.

Many players rely too strongly on linear momentum and ignore the potential for rotation or angular momentum for their shots. Ignore rotational acceleration and you limit your potential. To maximize power, use rotational force. The essence of all the sports we have examined so far is the creation of speed through rotation. As Kiegiel notes, the word *rotation* itself denotes circular movement. Because natural law teaches that the human body is engineered for circular motion and that any movement you make is circular in nature, any attempt you make to move a joint in a straight, or linear, manner violates natural law, inhibiting your flow.

You don't have to force rotational speed for more power. Your five major power sources—your legs, your hip girdle, your upper torso, your arms, and your wrists—provide all the energy you will ever need. But you must let all five sources flow together for a simultaneous release at impact. Any motion that jolts the flow ruins the proper speed, no matter how fast or slow the tempo required, of any movement.

To stroke a tennis ball effectively, you must control your body, head, shoulders, arm, wrist, and fingers. How to do this? Balance and awareness. Once you're balanced, while maintaining balance, use your hips for power. In jujitsu, you use your hips to throw your opponent. In tennis, you use your hips to stroke the ball. Utilize your hips to turn into the ball, while remaining balanced with your head still.

In baseball, Robson notes the following absolutes (fundamentals) of hitting:
- Dynamic balance controlling the center of gravity from start to finish; keeping strong posture
- Sequential rotation—using the body in the correct order, feetfirst, hands last.
- Axis of rotation
- Bat lag—pulling the bat through the zone as the last link in the swing[5]

These absolutes or fundamentals are nonnegotiable parts of athletic performance. Why are they nonnegotiable? Because they are governed by the natural law of physics. Each player may develop his own style, doing what feels natural and good for him, as long as he obeys the natural law of physics. Actually, an athlete should do what feels good, but not at the expense of absolutes or fundamentals. Develop style, staying within fundamental parameters.

Do the laws of physics, that is to say natural law, apply only to martial arts and baseball? Of course not! They apply to every sport; they apply to everything, including tennis. Malaska agrees that golf is dominated by physics. Physics is the law, not subject

---

[5] We agree with Robson about the fundamental necessity of lag, whether in the baseball, golf, or tennis swing. We talk about lag later in chapter 16 and assert that the lag should occur naturally. We believe *focusing* on lag may actually hinder performance.

to opinion. In physics or natural law, whatever you want to call it, the ball has to go where you hit it. When you hit a ball at a certain speed, angle, and spin, it is a mathematical certainty where that ball is heading.

Mike Malaska is right on when he says: "Physics is that good. Physics is perfect."

In baseball, Robson talks about one of the four fundamental absolutes of hitting as sequential rotation, that is to say using the body in correct order, feetfirst, hands last. Energy starts at the feet and works its way up through the body to the hands and the bat. The old saying "You're only as strong as your weakest link" still rings true.

The axis of rotation is important. Robson, as with the martial artists, talks about creating energy from "the feet to the fingertips," combining the idea of the axis of rotation with the kinetic chain. Connected with this is the need to keep the head on top of the hips throughout the entire swing. The closer the head is over the center of gravity, the belly button, the faster the body rotates. Conversely, the farther the head is from the "top" of the hips, the slower the body rotates.[6] Similarly, the closer the hands are to the body, the faster the body rotates.

In evaluating whether the body rotates faster the closer the hands are in, think of a figure ice skater doing the death twirl. The skater starts turning slowly with her arms out. Then as she increases speed, she continues to pull her arms in closer and closer to her body, spinning faster and faster, so that at the end, her body is a whirring blur. How does she do that? With physics. Athletes can do the same in other sports, whether in baseball, golf, martial arts, or tennis.

---

[6] As your parents and teachers told you in childhood, good posture is important!

In baseball, Robson observes that quick hands come only from quick rotation and good timing. How quickly the lower body rotates determines the bat speed. Therefore, start with the legs to get the bat through the zone faster. How fast the hands get the bat through the zone is the direct result of how fast the lower body rotates in sequence. Beginning the rotation aggressively is the only way to increase bat speed. Your hands are only so fast as your lower body allows.

How does one turn potential energy into usable energy? By transferring energy from the lower half of the body up to the hands and out to the bat head, golf club, or racket. To maximize energy transfer, linear movement (the stride) must stop before the hitter goes into rotational movement (swing). In this regard, the athlete transfers linear momentum to angular momentum, creating even more power.

In *Rope Burns*, trainer Mac McGee tells boxer Puddin' Pye that balance means leverage, leverage means speed, and speed means power. Because of this, balance and leverage, not muscle, provide speed and power.

Malaska sees much the same in golf, especially when looking at the separation of the lower and upper body. The body works in segments. Each body part accelerates and decelerates during the swing, with accelerating parts transferring power and momentum to the next part until the ultimate moment of impact.

Robson argues that the baseball hitter can be as aggressive as he wants to be as long as he keeps dynamic balance. He starts from the ground with his legs and hips, and while staying balanced and transferring linear momentum to angular momentum, with energy going from the ground through the body to the bat, he can attack the ball.

In golf, one of the most important parts of the game is how the feet pressure the ground. Your feet tell your knees, your hips, and your body how to move. So foot action and how you pressure the ground control your swing and its path. All tour players sequence from the ground to the knees to the hips to the midback, then they fire the shoulders, the arms, and the club.

We have just talked a lot about baseball, boxing, golf, the kinetic chain, and momentum. The principles inherent in swinging a baseball bat or golf club apply to tennis. Why are they the same? Because the laws of physics apply to everything.

Striking

Strike through the target. Many think of hitting at the target; instead think of hitting through the target so that you accelerate through the strike point. Boxing author F. X. Toole quotes legendary heavyweight champion Joe Louis as saying, "You don't punch your opponent, you punch *through* your opponent." In baseball, Robson notes that the hitter must maintain the axis of rotation and develop the rotational skills necessary to fire the bat through the hitting zone. In martial arts, for instance in breaking boards, one never hits at the board but instead strikes *through* the board. By hitting *at* a target, your mind stops *at* the target. By hitting *through* the target, your mind and, as a result, your body strike *through* the target with increased energy and power.

Trust Physics: Racket/Ball, Gun/Bullet

The racket and ball are like a gun and bullet. When shooting a gun, the bullet always goes straight. The bullet goes where the gun points. The same principle applies with tennis. If you tilt your shoulders and hit through the ball, the ball will go up. If you hit level through the ball, the ball will go forward through the court. Use physics. Set up balanced and aligned according to the situation, and good things will happen. Don't set up, and go off-balance, as physics will dictate a different, not so favorable, result.

Topspin

Let's talk about physics and topspin. Many players when hitting increased topspin make no additional adjustments. As a result, they hit the ball shorter in the court with little or no increased tactical advantage and with perhaps even decreased advantage. Why? Because they've ignored physics and common sense.

The natural physical consequence of topspin is to create a vacuum underneath the ball, which pulls the ball down. How does one utilize topspin's advantage of a heavier, differently bouncing ball? Use common sense. Hit the ball higher. Simply hit the ball higher. More height equals more depth.

We all recognize that more topspin is often better. How do we utilize simplicity and our biomechanical principles to hit deeper and with more topspin? Like throwing a ball over the fence, lower your body, your hips slightly move forward, which changes your spine angle. The shoulders are now tilting up. When you rotate, your body seeks equilibrium. The shoulders will naturally level out. Where your shoulders go, your arms follow; your racket and the ball will follow. To drive the ball through the court, simply start with your shoulders more level. It's the same as throwing a ball at a target right in front of you. Simple!

Strike through the Target and Finish

According to Robson, in baseball once you have your dynamic balance and have mastered the technique of transferring energy from the feet through the hands, then hitting through the ball is the only focal point. Make good contact by getting the bat through the middle of the ball.

Kiegiel notes in golf that the finish is an indicator of what happened through the swing. Our eyes are not good enough to see actual impact. The finish is evidence of what happened through the swing at impact. A flawed finish is a warning signal that something broke down earlier in the movement.

In martial arts, golf, baseball, and tennis, the finished product of physical motion reveals important clues to a player's effectiveness. This means that you must flow through impact with an effortless motion and allow your own athletic ability to play a significant role in your swing. Shoot for a smooth finish, no matter what sport or what stroke, and chances are that you will intuitively work out the kinks.

Remember:
Stroke
not at
but through the ball.
Think of the ball being in the way of your stroke
as you simply move the racket through.

CHAPTER FOURTEEN

STRATEGY AND TACTICS

In martial arts, the smart fighter will often defeat the more powerful or talented fighter. Robson notes in baseball that a smart hitter can outperform a more talented hitter. Perhaps even more often, the smarter tennis player will outperform and defeat a more powerful or talented opponent.

While each sport has its own sport-specific strategies and tactics, there are basics, fundamentals that flow throughout fighting and sport. Here we will identify the basic strategies for martial arts as applicable to other sports, and then focus on the specifics for tennis.

In martial arts, four basic strategies apply as follows:

1. Look for solutions, not problems.
2. Fight to your strengths and your opponent's weaknesses.
3. Get your opponent off-balance or distract him.
4. Go with the flow; don't fight force with force.
5. Vary your attack and style.

Look for Solutions, Not Problems

In every situation, in every attack, there are many solutions! Find the techniques that come naturally to you depending on your body type, personality, and comfort zone, whether they be joint locks, striking, throws, or combinations.

Fight to Your Strengths and Your Opponent's Weaknesses

You do not always fight someone of equal size and strength or those with the same fighting skills. Different opponents differ in their strengths and weaknesses. Learn and focus on your strengths. Learn and focus on your opponent's weaknesses and tendencies. Make your opponent fight to your strengths while you fight to your opponent's weaknesses; then you dramatically increase your survival odds.

Get Your Opponent Off-Balance or Distract Him

Work to expose your opponent's weaknesses. How? Get your opponent off-balance or distract him.

In martial arts, you want to turn your hips to move your opponent's head. The head is remarkably heavy, weighing usually ten to twelve pounds (four to five kilos). Just a little head movement will take a person off-balance. Move your opponent's head two inches and he's in trouble. Once your opponent loses balance, you control him.

Recognize how effective distraction can be. As boxing trainer Mac McGee schooled fighter Puddin' Pye in F. X. Toole's *Rope Burns*, deception is essential.

> Remember, if you want to hit him in the body, you go to the head first, that's to get him to lift his hands up, right? If you want to go to the head, hurt the body first to get the hands down. Trick him. Boxing is a game of lies.

Don't Fight Force with Force—Go with the Flow

Don't fight force with force; instead, use your opponent's force against him. As one sensei says, "If a train is coming down the tracks, get off the tracks!" Blend with the situation by using your opponent's force to your advantage.

The more your opponent does, the less you do. In martial arts, or anything for that matter, the tendency is for one to try to meet power with power, speed with more speed, or frantic activity with even more frantic activity. The opposite is more effective. The more your opponent tries to hit with power or offense, the less you hit with power or offense to counteract. This holds true in martial arts, and it also holds true in tennis.

Particularly with respect to fastballs in tennis, meet more with less. If someone hits a harder, faster shot, don't try to reply with more power. Instead, shorten up the stroke, keeping it simple. Just use your opponent's pace to redirect the ball back. Your opponent's fastballs mean less time for you. When you have less time, don't panic; don't get frantic. Just keep it simple, balanced, and under control.

Insecure people usually come in too strong. They try to intimidate or bully. Their anger and aggression do not have to affect you. Simply and calmly stay in the flow, using their force against them.

Vary Your Attack and Style

The fighter who varies his attack—for instance by changing between high and low attacks, moving quickly from defense to offense, changing rhythm, fighting with combinations, and doing the unexpected—are the hardest to fight. You just can't get comfortable and into rhythm with these fighters. These fighters are always pressuring, making you uneasy, and forcing you to utilize all your skills. Learn to do the same with your opponents.

Martial arts techniques distill physical motion and force into their purest essence, teaching you the most efficient manner in which to move and fight. As we've said, maximum force out of minimum motion, or pure ying and yang, that's what it is all about. Simplicity of movement, the rule of martial arts, is the very core of success.

These principles also go to the very core of athletic performance in general. Do these martial arts fundamentals apply to other sports, including baseball, golf, and most importantly for this book, tennis? You bet they do!

Tennis

To succeed at the highest level, you need pro strokes, but you also need pro smarts. Pro smarts consist of hitting the right shot at the right time. Pro shots are one thing; pro shot selection is another.

Hit Targets

Tennis is all about hitting targets. Targets don't move! It's just that most of the time, the target is either invisible or the open court, depending on how you perceive it. Don't stress about your opponent. Move to the ball, get balanced, and hit your target. Then do it again and again. Simple.

Yes, we've said "simple" again. Tennis is a beautiful paradox. What is simple is complicated, and what seems complicated often is remarkably simple.

This is why repetitions are so important. Practice, practice, practice; repetition, repetition, repetition. Hit target after target after target. Move your feet. Stay balanced. Work hard to keep it simple. Work hard to keep it easy. Aim at different targets with different spins, e.g., high, low, wide, deep, and short.

One might question whether hitting targets, practice, and the need for repetitions appropriately fall within the topic of tactics. Some think of tactics and strategy as something cerebral and thus complicated. Sometimes this *thinking* that something is more complicated actually makes it so, when it doesn't have to be.

Don't Miss

One day in an Istanbul tennis academy, a developing player complained after losing a tournament match that he did not feel he was getting enough tactical work in training. When asked why he thought he lost, he replied, "I missed too much." The coach's reply was, "Don't miss!" The value of tactics diminishes when a player can't keep the ball in play. In such a situation, the best tactic is "don't miss"! Tactics mean nothing if you can't hit the ball in. Conversely, the simple tactic of keeping the ball in will beat *almost everyone!* Day in and day out, perhaps the strongest, most effective tennis tactic is to hit the ball in. Sounds simple? It is.

Is your opponent beating you, or are you just missing your shots? Often it is the latter; you are missing and allowing your opponent to stay in the match. The solution: Don't miss.

If your opponent hits a winner, he hits a winner. Stay balanced. Control what you can control. Staying balanced and stroking as if you are catching and throwing make you a wall, at least as it appears to your opponent. Don't miss. Be a wall. Maintaining balance pressures your opponent by showing that you are in control and won't miss. This pressure forces more errors from your opponent as he tries for lower percentage shots with less margin of error.

Depth

Depth kills. Keep your balls deep and you immediately become a smarter technician. By keeping your shots deep in your opponent's court, you take away much, if not all, of his offensive firepower. It is amazing to observe the success that seemingly inferior ball strikers enjoy against "superior" players simply by keeping their balls deep.

Take Your Opponent Out of His Comfort Zone

The game of tennis revolves around your keeping your balance and staying in your comfort zone while working to get your opponent off-balance and out of his comfort zone. Work hard to set up and balance. Understand what takes your opponent off-balance. Understand what makes your opponent uncomfortable. Sometimes it is something so simple as to hit to the open court away from him so that he has to run, thus minimizing his chance to set up and balance. Sometimes, it is a weak shot in his arsenal or a flaw in his game. For instance, your opponent might have challenges with low-sliced balls, especially if he has a two-handed backhand.

Do what you can and move hard to stay within your comfort zone while doing what you can and working hard to take your opponent out of his comfort zone. Even if things are not working for you, find something your opponent doesn't like; try to take him out of his groove.

Set your patterns, then change them. Vary the speed, spin, and height of your shots. Try coming to net or staying back more.

Changing and varying the balls you hit can keep your opponent uncomfortable and out of rhythm. Take your opponent out of his comfort zone, and let doubt creep in.

Neutralize through the Middle

At the pro level, note how much players hit balls through the middle of the court. *Don't underestimate the utility of hitting through the middle!* Don't fear patience. Wait for your opportunity, and then change direction to open up the court. For impatient players, often mistakes are not the result of poor technique; rather, mistakes more often come from poor shot selection.

When in trouble, hit down the middle to neutralize. Still hit hard, but hit hard through the middle. Developing juniors will hit loopy balls to stay in the point, but as they mature and strengthen, they will need to learn to hit through the ball. The key is not to go for lines or low percentage shots but to simply hit through the center and live for another shot.

Aggressive play means going after the neutral or defensive balls that your opponent hits. Aggressive play does not mean going for off-balance winners. Even with "easier" balls, you still need to know when you're balanced and in position and when you're not. When not in position, when off-balance, or when the ball is not in your ideal hitting zone, hit back deep through the middle. Just this ability for patience is one of the key differences between hit-and-miss teen male testosterone-laden "macho gorilla" balls and the mature shot selection imbued in smarter professional play.

In moving up through the ranks, many junior players learn to hit crosscourt when on defense and under trouble. While this is certainly safer than hitting down the line, at the higher levels, hitting defensive crosscourt shots opens up the court for a reply down the line shot or a reply tight-angle crosscourt. Both of these reply options spell even more potential trouble for a player already on defense. Rather, the better option is to hit deep through the middle, minimizing the opportunity for both the tight crosscourt angle and the open down the line. Remember, depth remains key, as short replies will result in tight angles, an open court, and disaster, no matter where you are.

Green Light, Yellow Light, Red Light: Know Your Situation

When hitting the ball, a player is either in neutral, on offense, or on defense. When on defense, look to neutralize. When in neutral, *patiently* look for the offensive opportunity. When on offense, hit the ball.

Think of these situations as governed by a traffic light. If you are set up and balanced, be aggressive; go for your shot. If you're not completely set up and balanced, yellow light caution! Stay neutral with patience, waiting for your opportunity to go on the offensive. If you're scrambling and off-balance, red light danger, defense! Just do what you can to get the ball back with depth.

Too many players try for delusional winners when on defense, a tactic that makes a bad situation even worse. Stay smart. Know your situation. When on defense, obey the red light and just get the ball back. When neutral, stroke normally with depth and direction without going for too much; obey the yellow caution. When balanced and set up, green light! Go for your shot.

Baseline-to-Baseline Rallies

Previously we have talked about the need for depth with ground strokes. To hit deeper, hit higher over the net, preferably at least zone 2 (three feet / one meter over the net). In a baseline-to-baseline rally, *never ever* hit the ball into the net. Effective baseline rallies require net clearance and depth. A ball hit into the net would have been short in the court even if it had cleared the net. Hitting into the net is inexcusable. About the only time when hitting a ground stroke into the net is excusable is when passing the opponent at the net.

Move Forward to Take Time Away from Your Opponent and to Increase the Angle of Opportunity

Another example is court position, that is to say, where you are positioned in the court to stroke the ball. Let's again utilize common sense and physics. The closer you are to the net, the better the angle for hitting into the court. The closer you are to the net, the more options you have for controlling and beating your opponent. Conversely, the farther you are away from the net, the worse the angle for hitting into the court and the more limited the options for vanquishing your opponent.

From the baseline, you have an angle of about 20 degrees (out of 360) to hit into the court. Think of the perspective from the hitter's position on the court. If he were to turn around in a circle from where he is standing, he would turn 360 degrees. From the position, the tennis court comprises only about 20 degrees of the entire 360 degrees.

From that perspective, assuming your opponent is at midcourt, he only needs to cover 10 degrees in one direction and 10 degrees in the other. However, as you move closer to the net, the available angle of hitting, and conversely the angle of coverage for your opponent, increases dramatically, *so that by the point you get on top of the net, you have 120 degrees*. Furthermore, your opponent now needs to cover 60 degrees in one direction and another 60 degrees in the other direction. The message:

move closer to net to increase your angle of opportunity while also increasing your opponent's angle of coverage.

Moving forward provides another huge advantage—namely, it takes time away from your opponent. The more you move forward and the earlier you take the ball, the less time your opponent has to react. The less time he has to react, the more pressure he feels, and the more mistakes he will make.

Step forward to pressure your opponent by taking time away from him while simultaneously increasing your angle of opportunity. By moving forward, your opponent must cover more court in less time, thus increasing your chances of success.

The converse also rings true. While you want to move forward whenever you can, you also want to keep your opponent from moving forward to increase the angle against you and to take time from you. How do you do that? Hit deep. Hit with depth, and physics becomes your friend.

Passing Shots

Generally, when passing your opponent at net, keep the pass low, preferably in zone 1 (one foot / thirty centimeters) over the net. Rather than thinking about a clean pass with the first shot, instead hit through zone 1, even if it is at your opponent, and step in while anticipating a short volley. Volleyers tend to hit short on zone 1 volleys. Just anticipating the short volley makes you quicker. Often players hitting the passing shot look for the reactionary quick winner, which often ends with a "forced" error. Rather, play the two-shot combination with a zone 1 shot followed by the winner off the short volley. It is this type of percentage play that makes for "professional smarts."

Additionally, some opponents have quick hands. For those players, sometimes try hitting an off-pace zone 1 shot as they come in. Quick-handed opponents sometimes move too quickly, and slower balls put off their timing. Think of the slow zone 1 "pass" as like a changeup pitch in baseball.

Angles Beget Angles

When hitting angled shots, keep in mind that the natural reply is another angle. Angles beget angles. If you give an angle, expect an angle.

Look for the Down-the-Line Reply or Lob when Your Opponent Is Late

If your opponent is in trouble and late getting to the ball, look for the down-the-line reply or a lob. Earlier we talked about the need to neutralize through the middle when in trouble; however, many players don't play this smart. Look for the down-the-line, and chances are you will have an open court to hit into. Look for the lob and you'll have an overhead or swinging drive volley to finish the point.

Know Your Opponent's Tendencies

As we mentioned earlier, when pressured, humans naturally do what's comfortable. Tennis players are no different. Determine your opponent's favorite shots early and know that he will rely on those shots when he is under pressure, particularly when he is serving. Under pressure, people hit the shots they are comfortable with. No one likes to deal with pressure, so learn to apply pressure. When your opponent is under pressure, make him hit shots he doesn't want to hit. Also hit balls that go away from your opponent's tendencies, creating discomfort and even more pressure.

Change Losing Patterns and Keep Winning Patterns

Change losing patterns. Understand what is happening in a match. If you are losing, understand the patterns hindering you, and change. If you are winning, keep with what works, until your opponent forces you to change.

Know Yourself as Well as Your Opponent

Recognize that *everyone* gets nervous. As much as you want to be completely fearless, sometimes doubt creeps in. For those anxious moments, in golf, Malaska coaches one to know his "go to" shot. Whatever the sport, including tennis, practice a shot for when you get nervous, and then use it when those feelings of anxiety hit. Know and use your "go to" shot.

You Don't Need to Be Perfect

Recognize that you don't need to be perfect to succeed in tennis. If you win just 55 percent of the points, you'll win over 90 percent of the time!

Relax. If you're playing at the right level, your opponent will be good enough to win points from you. Don't worry! You don't need to win every point, so don't worry about winning every point.

Hit targets. Don't miss; keep the ball in. Keep the ball deep. Know your opponent's strengths, weaknesses, and tendencies; and take him out of his comfort zone. Neutralize by hitting deep through the middle. Move forward to take time away from your opponent while increasing your angle of opportunity. Change losing patterns, and keep winning patterns.

Stay smart. Know that if you can win 55 percent of the points, you almost certainly will win. Play smart to shave the odds in your favor. Stay calm and relaxed with the right attitude. Hit the right shot at the right time, and the odds will shift in your favor, even against a good opponent.

Remember:
Get the ball in; don't miss.
Keep the ball deep.
Stroke to different targets: high, low, wide, and deep.
Change speed and spin.
Set patterns and then change when your opponent starts to anticipate.

CHAPTER FIFTEEN

GENERAL PRINCIPLES OF STROKING IN TENNIS

Hit the Ball into the Court

There are five basic principles to stroking the ball. They are as follows:

1. Consistency—getting the ball in
2. Placement
3. Depth
4. Spin
5. Pace

These five factors follow the development of a player's strokes. Beginners must first learn to hit the ball in before they can even think about or deal with placement, depth, spin, and pace. Regrettably, many try to hit the ball hard and with pace before they learn to hit the ball in. This is symptomatic of the "macho gorilla" player and many, many teenagers with raging hormones. Before anything else, get the ball in.

From getting the ball in, learn to place the ball, to hit with directional intent. At this stage, learn to stroke the ball intentionally to different parts of the court.

As a player learns to place the ball, depth develops. The player starts to consistently keep the ball deep in the court.

As a player develops depth, he progresses to learning spin.

Finally, and preferably only after developing the first four components of consistency, placement, depth, and spin, does one learn to hit with pace.

Unfortunately, many players attempt to learn in the opposite manner. They may try to hit the ball with pace and spin, hoping that eventually they'll hit the ball in with placement and depth. This is a frustrating and long journey. The easier, more effective route is to follow the progression of first hitting in, then learning to place the ball, using directional intent. Then, after learning to hit the ball in with directional intent, learn to hit with depth. Then, and only then, should one focus on spin. Finally, after one has mastered the first four components, one can look to develop pace. By this point, one will probably not have to focus on pace. Pace develops naturally, almost automatically, as one masters the first four components of hitting in, hitting with direction, hitting with depth, and hitting with spin.

Hit Targets

Make your goal to set up and hit targets. *Not* to hit hard. *Not* to end the point. *Not* to hit away from your opponent. *Not* to win. Keep your motive and goal positive. Hitting the target is positive. Hitting hard, hitting to end the point, hitting away from your opponent, and hitting to win are negative goals. By looking to end the point or win the point on this shot, you take yourself out of the present and into the future, a classic example of negative-result-oriented thinking.

What do we mean by targets? We mean going for a specific area in the court, usually the open court. It does not mean trying to hit a specific object. Targets provide a focus of energy, which helps consistency and precision.

Stay in the present. Be specific and hit targets or spots on the court. When serving, toss to an imaginary target in the air. This assuredly helps steady and make your toss more consistent.

When stroking the ball, think of hitting a specific spot in the court.

Targets don't move! The Western mode of thought is too result oriented. Instead, stay within the process. Stay composed. Stay in the now. Stay positive. Look for solutions. Lose your ego and trust the physics of your shot.

Commit Physically and Mentally to the Shot with Balance

Commit physically and mentally before the shot, during the shot, and after the shot. Maintain balance *always*.

Make a Strong Unit or Core Turn on Each Shot

The first move on every shot is to turn the core and the hips. We call this the unit turn or core turn. Most players tend to first move with the arms and hands, which disconnects them from the ground and the rest of their body, depriving them of balance, strength, power, and control.

Turn the core. Turn the hips, keeping your arms in front of your body. Move from the core and the hips, and let the arms and hands go along for the ride. It is the core and hips that lead, with the arms and hands following. Many players do the opposite, to their severe detriment.

Know Where Your Racket Head Is

Know where your racket head is. Now this may seem fairly simple and self-evident. One may think, "What, do you think I'm an idiot? Of course, I know where my racket head is. It's at the end of the racket, which I'm holding in my hand."

The fact is that many are not fully aware of their racket head in relation to their body and the oncoming ball. It is this kinesthetic awareness that one must maintain *at all times!* For instance, some players, including lower-level professionals, may "lose" control of their racket face on the take back and through the beginning of the stroke, thus losing the ability to solidly contact the ball with control.

The simpler your stroke is, the easier it is to control and know where the racket head is. Obviously, you can't look at the racket head as you stroke because you've got an oncoming ball to deal with. Instead, work to kinesthetically sense and *feel* the racket head.

Keep a Loose Grip

As we've mentioned earlier, almost all tennis players grip their racket much too tightly. On a relative scale from 1 to 10, with 1 as the loosest grip and 10 the tightest, try for a 3 level tightness grip. Most players report a normal grip of a 5, 6, or 7. Loosening to a 3 level allows for better feel and more acceleration. A looser grip allows the racket to do its work. Conversely, a tighter grip inhibits acceleration, power, and racket-head speed.

Catching and Throwing

Move and load for your ground strokes as if you're catching the ball. Keep a wide base with the shoulders squarely level and the back straight, perpendicular to the ground. Always stay balanced. Then unload through the ball as if you're throwing the racket over the net at a target in front of you. Feel as if you're releasing the racket (but of course, don't let go).

If you want more height or depth, tilt your shoulders, changing your spine angle, as if you are throwing the racket toward the top of the fence behind your opponent. To help tilt your shoulders, shift your hips forward toward the net. By doing this, your shoulders and spine naturally will tilt and aim higher, just like throwing a ball over a fence.

Actually go into a field sometime and practice throwing an old racket. Throwing a racket will help give you the correct feel for ground strokes, serves, and overheads. We're serious. Throwing and stroking are much the same.

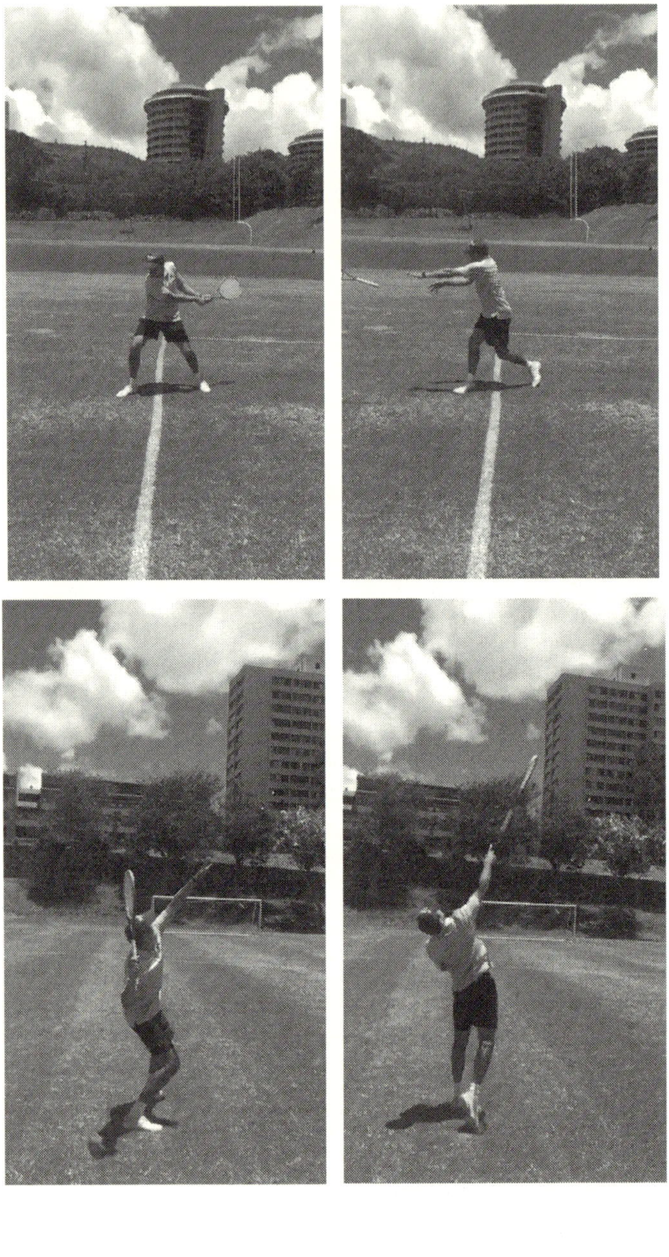

Check out the pictorial sequences later in the chapters on the forehand (chapter 16), backhand (chapter 17), and serve (chapter 19), which all demonstrate throwing as stroking.

Keep the Hands in the Handshake Position

As mentioned earlier, a basic athletic position of strength is the handshake position. The same rings true for all tennis strokes. Keep the handshake position through contact, and you'll help maximize the use of your entire body through the shot.

Contact the Outside of the Ball

Make initial contact with the outside of the ball.[7] This is a factor often ignored or overlooked. Yet it is vitally important for natural topspin and weight.

By first touching the "outside" of the ball, the racket's path will naturally come back through the ball, producing more spin and power. What is the "outside"? It is the part of the sphere that is farther away from the body. For a right-handed player on the forehand, the outside of the ball is on the right; on the backhand, the outside is on the left. In thinking of the ball as a clock face, for a right-handed forehand, the outside is around four o'clock, with the backhand being around eight o'clock.

---

[7] Think about what happens in a tennis stroke when the racket and ball come together. Before contact, the ball and racket are independent forces on intersecting paths. When the two forces come together, at some finite point the ball and racket first touch. While studies show that the human eye and brain's perception are too slow to see the actual time when the ball meets the racket, the fact remains that it does actually occur, and the eye/brain *can* see the general part of the ball that the racket first contacts.

Common sense dictates that when the racket and ball first collide, initial contact must occur at some point on the ball. Make that point the outside of the ball.[8]

Many don't initially understand what the outside of the ball is, much less the necessity for making initial contact there. Beginners, for instance, often are astounded that the focus on the ball can be this specific. Often a beginner will say, "Hit the outside of the ball? Heck, I'm fortunate to touch the ball at all!" More advanced players often are so caught up with everything else that is going on that they forget about the critical point when the racket and ball actually meet. Yet, without contact, everything else falls apart!

Some players might ask, "If I want to hit through the ball, why shouldn't I make contact at the back of the ball [around six o'clock]?" Why? Because, while many players think of the typical stroke as going straight forward, in fact the normal stroke follows an arc as the arm and racket go through the ball and follow through. The arm is going to stay connected to the body; hence, as it strokes, it will move in an arc from the side around the body. Therefore, by making first contact with the outside of the ball, one takes advantage of this natural arc as the racket naturally goes *through* the ball.

Try it. Focus on the exact point where the racket first touches the ball. See what happens when the racket first touches the outside. See the natural topspin. As you practice this more and more, you'll develop natural heavy topspin.

---

[8] We are talking about the overwhelmingly large majority, perhaps 90 percent of shots. There are some shots, notably the inside-out forehand, for which the proper contact is the "inside" of the ball. As we mention later in our discussion of the inside-out forehand, there is some debate as to whether one actually hits the true "inside" of the ball or just less than normal of the "outside" of the ball.

Hitting the outside of the ball accentuates spin and weight. Even when slicing the ball, try making initial contact with the outside of the ball. Hitting the outside of the ball magnifies spin, even slicing spin.

Maximum Speed through the Point of Impact

Let's deal with a little common sense here. We've talked about setting up. We've talked about flow. We've talked about physics, including angular momentum, ground force, the kinetic chain, and simple, efficient, effective movement. What does this all point toward? Answer: It points to generating increased racket-head speed to stroke the tennis ball with more power and more control. Yes, we want more racket-head speed, because racket-head speed provides the force that allows us to play better. Knowing this, keep in mind that there is only one time when you need to generate maximum racket speed, and that time is through the point of impact. Generating maximum racket-head speed at any other time is irrelevant and meaningless. Work your stroke so that you maximize racket-head speed through contact, and then allow the flow to decelerate through the follow-through.

Stroke through the Ball as if Along the Level Plane of a Table

Hit through the equator/center of the ball on almost all your shots. Keep hitting level *through* the ball. Imagine a table and hit along the level tabletop's plane. When positioned inside the baseline, for higher balls with the contact point above hip-to-shoulder height, hit level along the imaginary tabletop, but close the racket face. For short balls below waist level, tilt your hips and shoulders. As you turn and stroke through the ball, your shoulders will naturally level out from the tilt. By tilting the shoulders, you almost cannot hit the ball into the net (provided you keep your head still).

Keep Your Head "Inside" Your Feet

Balance, balance, balance—it's all about balance. How do you keep your balance? Keep your head "inside" your feet. In other words, keep your head on top of your body, over your shoulders, over your hips, and thus over and inside your feet. In martial arts, the objective is to get your opponent's head outside his feet, which invariable pulls him off-balance, putting him in danger. The same principle applies to tennis. Work to stay on balance while getting your adversary off-balance. Keep your head "inside" your feet. Move from your center. Then hit the shot that takes your opponent off-balance and out of his comfort zone.

Stay Low on All Shots

Stay low on all strokes. Keep the back straight with the hips low. Keep the hips active while your upper body stays passive. There are two ways to get low. The first is to bend your knees and lower your legs. The second is simply to widen your stance. For many, bending the knees takes more strength and energy. For these people, simply widening the stance gives much the same stability. Either way, work to stay low on all shots.

Turn the Hips Faster and Let the Rest Follow

The faster you turn your hips, the heavier your ball becomes. Turn the hips and let the rest, including your arms and racket, follow. How do you turn the hips on as many balls as possible? The answer: Move your feet. Move your feet to set up in the right place so that you can fire your hips through the ball. Turn your hips and let the rest follow.

Feel the Ground beneath Your Feet

Feel the ground. Always. Feel the ground when you move. Feel the ground when you set up. Feel the ground when you stroke as you push off the earth. This is the ground force of martial arts, and it also applies to tennis.

Once you lose the feel of the ground, you lose ground force, breaking the kinetic chain. Once you lose the feel of the ground, your stroke becomes an arm stroke, with less power and less control. Always load on the back leg / power leg, pressing the back foot into the ground as if digging into sand to drive off.

Depth Kills

Generally, the deeper into the court you hit, the better you perform. Want to hit deeper? Hit higher over the net. Keep the following formula in mind:

$$NC = D$$
(net clearance equals depth)

To hit higher, simply tilt your shoulders and hit through the ball normally. You don't need to lift your body or jump. In fact, *do not lift your body*! Just stay balanced and tilt your shoulders.

Which hurts more, depth or speed? Answer: Depth.

1. Depth kills.
2. Depth forces errors.
3. Depth takes away angles, effectively making your court smaller for your adversary while making his court bigger. Again, physics at work and physics in play.

In working with net clearance, think of three zones above the net. Zone 1 is approximately one foot / thirty centimeters over the net. Zone 2 is approximately three feet / one meter over the net, while zone 3 is a lob. Use zone 2 for the normal baseline-to-baseline shot, saving zone 1 for passing shots when the opponent is at net.

For Spin, Rotate Your Body through the Ball with Initial Contact on the Outside of the Ball

Many players try to brush up on the ball to hit spin. While one can hit lots of spin by "brushing" up on the ball, these types of shots provide glancing blows without significant weight or power. The better approach to develop spin is to set up correctly, turning the body through the ball with initial contact on the outside of the ball. By making contact on the outside of the ball, the racket naturally goes through the ball, producing natural spin.

Shorten the Radius for More Spin— Short Crosscourt Angle Shot

To get more spin, you don't need to work your hands over the ball as much; instead, just shorten the radius of your swing by feeling your elbow stop by your side. The racket will accelerate through the shot. Shortening the radius of the swing quickens racket-head speed. For example, imagine a ball tied to a string revolving around an axis. If you stuck your finger in the middle to shorten the axis, the ball would increase its rotations per minute (rpm). Similarly, rotating from the elbow shortens the radius of the stroke, thus effectively allowing more rpm and spin on the ball, allowing for effective spin.

In shortening the radius, stroke as if your other arm is catching your forearm. Stay loose; don't muscle the ball. Let the forearm go through. By shortening the radius this way, kinetic energy will flow and release through the wrist into the hand, racket, and through the ball.

The short, tight angle crosscourt shot is an underused but wickedly effective shot. Even if not an outright winner, the tight angle takes the opponent off the court, often setting up a succeeding winner to the open court. Adding the short angle crosscourt adds a valuable dimension to one's game.

Let the stroke do its work. Fight the temptation to jump. Stay down. Stay level. Don't lift. Just shorten the radius and let the racket go through the ball.

High Deep Balls and Low Balls—Shorten the Radius

This idea of shortening the radius applies not only to sharp angle shots but also high deep balls that you want to hit back through the court with a high trajectory and high bounce, and for low balls when you want to hit back through the court.

Deep Fastballs

Stay balanced when setting up for the deep fastball, lowering the hips and widening the base. Keep the back straight and shoulders level. Turn through the ball in a quick 1-2 rhythm, finishing with the hands below the waist.

One analogy is to think of the fire drill commandment, "Stop, drop, and roll." Stop and stay balanced. Drop by lowering your legs and hips. Then roll by turning and staying low through the ball. Do this correctly and the ball will go deep through the opponent's court, deflecting up on the rise.

High Balls

High balls are the bane of many players. They feel that they just can't effectively stroke and must somehow jump or lunge to get up to the high balls. Not so. Start low and try to stay low for as long as you can.

On balls played behind the baseline, 90 percent of the time, tilt your shoulders and spine, letting your lower body rotate through the ball on the stroke. Your hand will feel as if you are "on" the ball for an extended time.

On high balls taken inside the baseline that come up on the rise between your waist and shoulders, *keep your balance*. With high balls, as with everything else, maintaining balance is paramount. Keep your shoulders level. Stay low. Fight the urge to jump. Rather than tilt the shoulders or jump, simply close the racket face and hit through the ball. In closing the racket face, think of catching a high ball. How do you catch a high ball? Answer: With your palm down. Do the same with the racket face when hitting a high ball. Load on your back leg, rotate your hips, and keep your palm down.

Low Balls

Drop the handle down, then while holding the racket in the handshake position, drop your forearm. Lower the hips and tilt your shoulders with your hips closer to the net than your head. Keep a wide base. Stay down and rotate your hips, finishing low with the head still. In other words, get low and stay low.

When keeping the spine perpendicular for lower balls, feel as if you're sinking into the ground.

Running Shots

On running shots, tilt your shoulders with the hips closer to the net than your head. For more spin, wait a split second to hit just a bit later. Widen your stance and whip the racket through the ball. To whip, you can shorten the radius as previously described.

Pete Sampras used to hit running forehands seemingly effortlessly. Using a baseball analogy, think of an infielder taking a wide groundball and making a running throw. Have you noticed how easy and relaxed the throw seems to flow? Do the same with your running shots in tennis. Don't panic. Don't overhit. Just let it flow, letting the racket go through the ball as if you are flipping a Frisbee.

If you were running around the track and someone asked you to throw your racket to the center of the field as you ran by, you would slightly tilt your shoulders, then turn and release the racket. You wouldn't jump or over-rotate. Do the same with your running shots in tennis. Play as an athlete.

Transition/Approach Shots

We've just talked about feeling the ground with your feet. Often with transition shots, the player rushes toward the net, ignoring his all-important balance and setup. Keep your balance with your transition shots. Use your body, set up, feel the ground, and turn through the ball. Let the hips and the turn through the ball do the work, not the hands.

On approach shots, many players tend to lean forward on their front foot, a habit that impedes power and makes the player lose balance. Make sure instead that your weight initially is on your back leg so that you can drive through the ball better. Try to feel as if you're stopping on your back leg as you stroke the approach shot. Too many do almost the opposite by trying to move forward through the ball, causing them to hit too early, thus pulling them off-balance. Instead, stay biomechanically strong by "stopping" with your weight on the back leg and stroking through the ball.

Five Different Balls—Same Principles

There are five different balls:
1. High short balls
2. Fast deep balls
3. Volleys
4. Half volleys
5. Returns

On all these,
1. keep the buttocks low,
2. keep the spine perpendicular,
3. keep the shoulders level and on line with the target,
4. keep a wide base,
5. keep the chin up, and
6. hit level through the ball.

Always stay balanced. To minimize lift, stay down and low, hitting just a bit later.

Remember:
Stay low.
Load from the ground.
NC = D (net clearance = depth)
Hit through the equator of the ball.
Where your shoulders go, your arms go!
Tilt your shoulders for more height and depth.

CHAPTER SIXTEEN

THE FOREHAND

Grip—between Eastern and semi-Western. The grip within this range provides the potential to hit with the optimal mix of spin and power. Many young players learn their forehand with the Western grip, a grip that could well inhibit development as they mature, growing bigger and stronger. This is not to say that one cannot play at a high level with the Western grip; one can. It's just that the potential to develop increases with a more "reasonable" grip, for instance, the potential to hit flatter balls when needed and unleashing the biomechanical advantage in elevating the elbow (something difficult with a severe Western grip).

Teaching and developing a grip within these parameters must occur early developmentally. Grips are a tricky thing, and if a mature player has already developed his stroke with an extreme Western grip, chances are that changing to a grip within the recommended parameters could do more harm than good. Grips, particularly forehand grips, become ingrained habitually at an early age and are difficult to change.

Thus, with young players, teach and develop the grip within the recommended parameters from the Eastern to the semi-Western grip. Remain very, very careful with older, more advanced players, including experienced teenagers when considering changing from a Western grip. Often, the better course is to just leave the grip alone, even though suboptimal, as the odds are that the grip and habit are too ingrained and established.

Traditionally, most coaches and players have learned the forehand grip with an emphasis on where the *V* between the thumb and forefinger is located on the racket handle. We believe that a better, more functional reference point is the location of the butt of the hand. The butt of the hand should be behind the racket, not under the racket as with the Western grip, or over the racket as with the Continental grip.

With the butt of the hand behind the racket, the player has more racket stability and support. Also, he strengthens the kinetic chain, allowing the hand and arm the position to keep the elbow up, thus providing for a better kinetic load. With the butt of the hand over or under the racket with the Continental or Western grips, the player cannot get or keep the elbow up, thus hindering an effective kinetic chain. Get the butt of the hand behind the racket, and the grip should function almost optimally.

Unit turn. We see many players coming who start the forehand by taking the hands back rather than first turning the shoulders. This initial move, if not corrected, limits the player's potential. Focus on a shoulder and midbody turn, which automatically moves the arm and racket back. One common diagnostic observation for someone who does not have a strong unit turn is that he will move the hands with the elbow down.

Elbow away from body. This ties in with the unit turn but is separate. Many, particularly young girls, have difficulty with the strength to get the elbow up and out. Monitor your developing players and push them into this parameter as they develop their strength. The elbow position provides a valuable link in the forehand's kinetic chain from the shoulder through the arm, the wrist, and into the racket. While the unit turn helps ensure that the core and shoulders keep engaged, keeping the elbow out works to extend leverage, optimizing the kinetic chain through the arm.

Racket head over hand on take-back. Racket-head speed is the key to developing effective powerful shots. The straight-back, linear back swing, while easier to get the racket on faster and harder hit balls, does not provide optimal racket-head speed. By taking the racket head back over the hand, one essentially loads the racket to drop down with angular momentum roller-coaster style, generating more acceleration and racket-head speed.

Use of stances—open, semi-open, square. Frankly, with the development of so much power in today's game, one must be able to hit with every stance. The key is in getting to the ball with a balanced setup however you can, whether the forehand stance is open, semi-open, or square. Given this, players should practice hitting off either foot and with every stance. Having said this, there are some guiding principles as to which stance to use in which situation. Tend to hit more open stance when defensive and pushed back, when neutral generally hit semi-open stance. When moving forward offensively, the square stance is often most effective.

Hands through ball. Particularly at the higher levels, the ability to continually adjust occurs with the feet and the hands. The human body, the brain, and the ways they coordinate are amazing, continually processing sensory information, seemingly with each passing millisecond. In hitting a tennis ball, even with perfect preparation and technique, the player must continually adjust. At the moments just before and during contact, the sense or feeling of taking the hands through the ball and contact is critical. Often it is this ability, sometimes seemingly innate, that separates the gifted from the mediocre.

Finish. The finish maintains the shot's flow as one takes the hands through the ball. The finish is not a set follow-through. Given the range and pace of balls, particularly at the top level, one must take the racket through the ball at different heights and contact points. The key is not where you finish, whether it is over the shoulder or around the waist; the key is that you finish.

Recently, others have made much at the professional level about the forehand "lag." The lag occurs after the initial load when the stroke flows down through the stroke toward impact. As the racket heads toward impact, the wrist and racket "lag" behind the hand, forming a kind of cocking action. Some coaches now teach their players to consciously lag the racket before impact.

While we agree that the lag occurs and is important, we disagree that a player needs to focus on it. With a smooth, balanced, flowing shot, the lag occurs *naturally*. Actively focusing on the lag can actually hinder the shot's flow and power. As part of a flowing sequential rotation, the lag occurs naturally. Rather than focus and consciously try for the lag, just let it happen as you use your body to generate the stroke!

Treat the forehand as a throw. Most people relax when throwing, even when trying to throw something a long distance. Imagine or try throwing something a long way. Think of how you feel when going through the throwing motion. Most people stay relaxed throughout the motion. If you can do this with a throw, try doing the same thing with your forehand. Don't worry about where the ball goes; instead, relax as if you are throwing, and just let the racket flow through the ball.

Core turn with body, *not the arms*, taking the racket back.

Stroke starts from the ground up. Note the
body turn, also lowering for balance and power,
keeping an aggressive attitude and feeling.
The back foot digs into the ground. The body unwinds
naturally from the foot, knee, hips, core, shoulders,
and arm into the racket and through the ball.

Let the lag occur naturally by relaxing the body, letting the bigger muscles do the work, all the while keeping loose fingers on the racket (3 tension on a scale from 1 to 10). Note that the elbow stays in front of the body throughout the stroke.

Keep energy focused *through*, never at, the target, keeping natural extension and staying on balance through the finish. Keep balance always—before, during, and afterward!

While beginners, for very good reasons, often hit the ball too late and need to learn to make contact earlier and more in front, many advanced players actually make contact too far in front. By focusing too much on making contact in front, advanced players often unintentionally take themselves off-balance by almost lunging forward. Instead, the advanced player will hit a more effective forehand by balancing as if to catch and simply turning through the ball. It's almost as if one is waiting to catch the ball, only to turn through the ball with the entire body.

Inside-Out and Inside-In Forehands

The inside-out and inside-in forehands are forehands where one almost runs around the backhand side to stroke a forehand instead of a backhand. The inside-out forehand goes from one's backhand side of the court crosscourt to the other side; the inside-in forehand goes from the same position down the line.

The keys in stroking either stroke are the same, but for one difference: the contact point. First, move to get around the ball. Set up with your weight low on your back leg and your hands in front of your body. Then turn through the ball, keeping the hands still, and making contact with the "inside"[9] of the ball. Making

---

[9] There's some debate as to whether one actually contacts the true "inside" of the ball, or just less of the "outside" of the ball. The debate may just be a different perspective on the contact point, as the point of reference in differentiating "outside" and "inside" can change as one moves and turns to hit a spherically shaped ball. From solely the baseline perspective looking straight ahead to the other baseline, one hits the inside of the ball; however, from the player's perspective, one still hits the outside of the ball, as the player has moved around and turned to hit the inside-out shot. What is "outside" to one when referring to a sphere is "inside" to another, depending on their literal point of view and stance. Whatever the perspective, there is no debate that one must hit *through* the ball in executing both the inside-out and inside-in forehands.

contact with the inside of the ball produces a natural angle of deflection. The ball goes where the racket face faces at impact.

All too often, players rush inside-out and inside-in forehands, going off-balance by transferring their weight too soon to the front leg. Relax. Stay on your back leg and, keeping your hands still, just turn through the inside of the ball. In staying on your back leg, feel as if you're stopping. This is how you get the balance to turn through the shot.

On low balls, fight the urge to change your normal stroke. Instead just tilt your shoulders more while staying down and balanced on the back leg. Tilting the shoulders gives the necessary lift; furthermore, as the body rotates through the shot, the shoulders will naturally even out, giving a proper trajectory to the ball up and over the net but inside the court.

Stroke the inside-in forehand precisely the same as the inside-out shot, with only one difference: contact the "outside" of the ball instead of the "inside." Contacting the outside provides a different angle of deflection that takes the ball to the other side of the court.

Remember:
The hips take the racket back,
not the arms.
The racket is an extension of the body,
following the unit/hip turn and release.
The forward stroke starts from the ground,
going through the feet,
knees,
hips,
core,

*shoulders,
elbow from the inside (causing natural lag),
hand,
and racket.
Do not "hit" the ball.
Instead, throw the racket through
the ball to a specific target!*

CHAPTER SEVENTEEN

THE BACKHAND

As we've mentioned before, ground strokes are like throwing. As with the forehand, treat the backhand stroke as a throw, and let it flow.

Core turn with body, *not the arms*, taking the racket back.

Beginning power sequence, lowering with
the back foot digging into the ground.

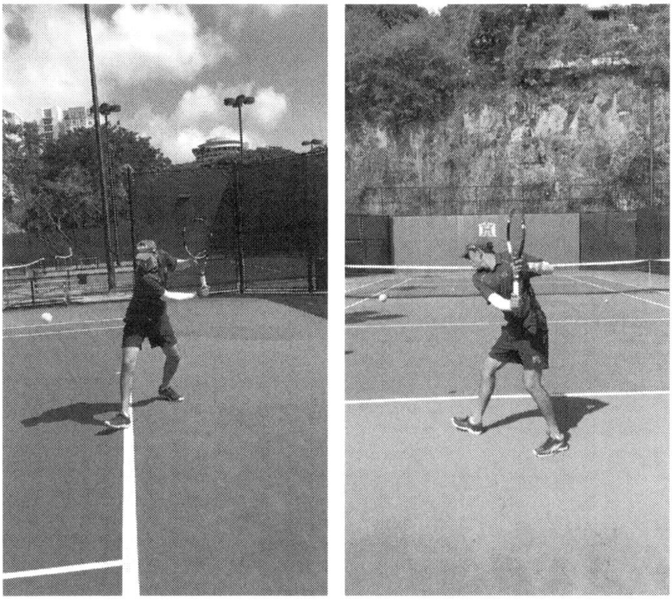

Arms lag *naturally* from the body loading and unloading. Never do the arms "consciously reach back." Instead, as the body moves forward, the racket moves *naturally* in the other direction, lagging to the inside.

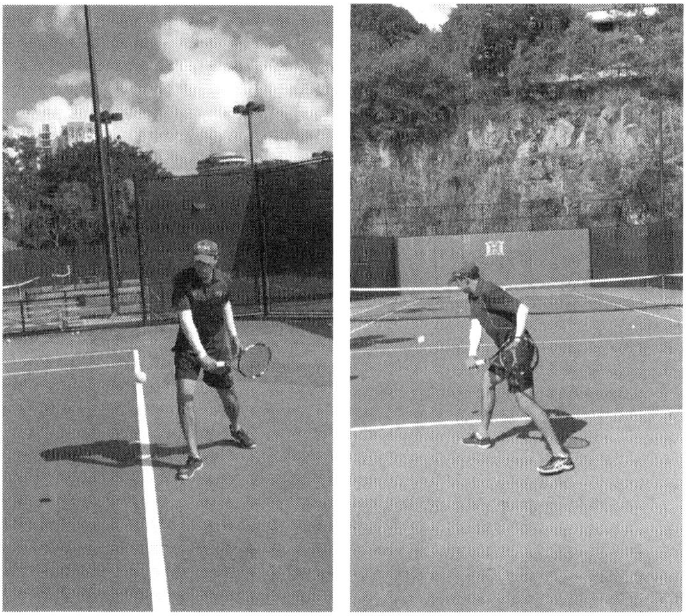

Natural release *through* the target with balance and aligned body.

Grip—two hand: bottom-hand Continental to Eastern forehand grip. For right-handers, the bottom hand is the right hand. In the "old days," the two-handed backhand was essentially a one-handed shot assisted by the nondominant hand to provide strength and stability. As such, the dominant bottom hand used the traditional one-handed Continental or Eastern backhand grip. The game has now changed so that the two-handed backhand is basically a left-handed shot. Given this change, the dominant bottom-hand grip should now be the Continental to Eastern *forehand*, which allows the left hand to become more dominant and go through the ball more.

Grip—two hand: top-hand Eastern to semi-Western. Because today's two-handed backhand is primarily a nondominant left-handed shot, the top hand (left hand) should utilize the Eastern to semi-Western forehand grip. This grip allows the left hand to dominate and accelerate more through the ball.

Grip—one handed: Eastern grip. Generally utilize the Eastern grip; for more topspin for right-handers, move the knuckles to the right a bit (obviously lefties move their knuckles to the left).

Unit turn. As with the forehand, focus on a shoulder and midbody turn that automatically moves the arm and racket back.

Racket head over hand on take-back. As with the forehand, racket-head speed is key to developing effective, powerful shots. The straight-back, linear back swing, while easier to get the racket on faster and harder hit balls, does not provide optimal racket-head speed. By taking the racket head back over the hand, one essentially loads the racket to drop down with angular momentum roller-coaster style, generating more acceleration and racket-head speed.

Hooking the elbow back. We often see a difference between the women's two-handed backhand and the men's. While many men have a straight-back approach, almost all the top women's two-handed backhands have the left elbow hooking back. This provides valuable additional angular momentum by developing a circular motion when the elbow hooks back, down, and through the ball, much different than the simple straight-back approach that is primarily a linear motion.

Why the difference between the men and the women? One, the men can often get away with it. Men are stronger. Additionally, the men's game generally revolves around the forehand. The backhand is normally a neutral or defensive shot. If a man has the time and opportunity to hit offensively, he generally will run around the ball to hit a forehand. At the professional level, men are faster and cover more court, to the extent that about 70 percent of all their shots are forehands. In the women's game, the lack of inherent speed (compared to men) means that forehands and backhands are about evenly split, fifty-fifty. Given this, the backhand is just not as important to the men's game as the women's. While men can "get away" with a weaker shot, women have to maximize whatever biomechanical advantages they can develop with the backhand. As a result, with the top-level women's game, backhands are technically and biomechanically better than the men's. Does this mean that a male player should not focus on his backhand? Not at all. This discussion merely explains the general factual disparity between the male and female pro backhand. While many men's backhands are so ingrained and habitual that to make any changes could work more harm than good, at the younger and developmental levels, the player—whether a male or female—should incorporate the elbow hook. Just because someone "can get away with it" does not mean that one should give up the cause to improve. Even in the men's game, why not develop a potential weapon on the backhand side, just in case you need it?

Use of stances: open, semi-open, square. As discussed with the forehand with today's power game, one must be able to hit with more than one stance. Balance points and feeling where your body is at contact are critical. Too many players hit their backhand with only one stance, thus limiting their effectiveness. When you have time, get your back leg behind the ball and step into it linear fashion with the front leg. When you don't have time, particularly on wide or deep balls, don't be afraid just to hit off your back leg and turn through the ball. This helps not only with the shot itself, but also with recovery footwork as you move back into the court after the shot.

Hands through ball. See the above discussion on hands through the ball on the forehand. The same reasons apply to the backhand.

Finish. See the above discussion on hands through the ball on the forehand. The same reasons apply to the backhand.

One-handed backhand like throwing a Frisbee. A one-handed backhand is very similar to throwing a Frisbee. Lower your body on your back leg while loading or turning back into your back leg. Feel the torque and unwind from the ground up. Keep the upper body passive. On the one-handed backhand, your shoulders remain more sideways, so the upper body remains facing the side fence.

Two-handed backhand like a left-handed forehand. For a right-handed player, the two-handed backhand is similar to a left-handed forehand. Let the ball get between your feet, rotate your hips, and let the upper body follow the rotating lower body. You will finish with the upper body facing the net more.

Remember:
The hips take the racket back,
not the arms.
The racket is an extension of the body,
following the unit/hip turn and release.
The forward stroke starts from the ground,
going through the feet,
knees,
hips,
core,
shoulders,
elbow from the inside (causing natural lag),
hand,
and racket.
Do not "hit" the ball.
Instead, throw the racket through
the ball to a specific target!

CHAPTER EIGHTEEN

THE VOLLEY, OVERHEAD, AND DROP SHOT

THE VOLLEY

Continental grip. While the grip remains the same with the volley, the hand's pressure points on the racket handle change from forehand to backhand. Some may think of this as a change in grip, when in reality the change is in the pressure point. For the forehand, the pressure point is the hand's maw, below the pinky finger's base. For the backhand, the pressure point is the hand's maw at the thumb's base.

Ready position toward backhand side. When asked to take the ready position, many players will get ready with both hands on the racket, elbows in front and with the racket face perpendicular to the body and the opponent. Instead, hold the racket face slightly open to the backhand side, thus allowing for a quicker reaction on a ball hit straight at the body.

Limited backswing. Almost all players swing too much on their volleys. Keep it simple. Generally, intercept the path of the ball with your racket and almost block the ball, so that you almost have the sense of the ball just bouncing off the racket.

Slightly open racket face. Believe it or not, good volleys generally have a trajectory. They are not hit straight down into the court. Keep your racket face slightly open so as to allow for net clearance and depth into the court.

Feeling ball with hands. Don't hit the volley; instead, "feel" it on the racket. "Feel" may consist of relaxing the hands to soften the racket at impact. Many players may not initially understand the idea of "feel." This is understandable as the idea is necessarily a kinesthetic concept. Most people's learning styles are more centered on seeing or hearing. One cannot see or hear "feel"; one can only feel "feel." So for a person whose learning style is primarily visual or aural, the idea of feel may provide a bit of a disconnect.

Having said this, how do we develop feel on our volleys? Try to think of "absorbing" the ball on the racket, then try to time your increased pressure in the hands at contact to redirect the ball either deep, short, with angle, soft, or hard. Keep the feet, legs, and body balanced.

On the volley, face the ball with your body and keep balanced, with your back straight, shoulders level, butt down, and head straight. Make the first move with the hips, moving from the center. Keep the wrist in the handshake position for even more stability. Get the feel of volleying with the legs rather than with the arms. Most players volley short because they don't use their legs.

Most often try for too much on their volleys. What is essentially a simple shot becomes an immense effort to produce a winning thing of beauty, a testament to the volleyer's superior athletic ability and innate competitive drive. Alas, this common delusion of grandeur with respect to a simple shot often ends in failure.

Rather than approach the volley as an opportunity to show your unparalleled superiority on the court, keep it simple. Make the shot. Keep your balance. Keep your elbows in front, *always!* For balance, move from your center, turning your shoulders so your sternum always faces the ball. Too many players make the mistake of reaching with their arms on the volleys. Rather than reach, move from the body, with your back straight and chin up. Keep your shoulders level with your sternum facing the ball.

Catch the ball with the racket face open, making contact through the outside of the ball if possible.

Turn with the hips, *always* keeping the arms in front of the body. Widen the stance and lower the body. Move with the center of the body, maintaining balance with a straight back and the chin up.

Simply stated, move with the center (think hips) of your body, rather than just with the arms, while always keeping balanced. Use the legs to move the body forward into the ball. When possible, move with the outside leg first, driving the front leg forward toward the ball. This helps one stay behind the ball with balance and strong legs.

A great example of moving with the sternum rather than the arms is the YouTube video showing Cara Black volleying with rapid fire on a wall. Check the video at https://www.youtube.com/watch?v=ZjKgM6huV_A.

Critical to the volley (and most shots for that matter, other than the serve) is the split step. Many players either split step late or don't split step at all. The split step is essential as you balance and prepare for your opponent's next shot. Here's a tip for the split step on the volley: when your opponent starts to hit, widen your base and balance. This allows you to prepare yourself on time, maximizing your chances of volleying effectively. Widen your base and balance; good things will happen.

Keep your shoulders level. Once the shoulders dip, you tend to go off-balance, the ball goes down, and bad things happen.

Keep the chin up. Once the chin drops, the head drops, pulling you off-balance. As we've mentioned before, the head is surprisingly heavy. Always keep the head balanced on top of the shoulders. Maintain balance and erect posture. Move your head, and your balance shifts automatically, whether you want or not. Keep your chin up, and your head stays still, allowing for better balance.

When you have time, move forward as if to catch. When moving forward, you come closer to the outside of the ball, giving a better angle into the court. Just this technique alone helps minimize errors. No matter how good we are or how much we practice, we cannot always hit cleanly. With the wrist in the handshake position, keeping the racket in front, with the bottom edge leading (creating a more open face) as you move to the ball, minimizes errors, even on those inevitable off-center hits.

On the backhand side, keep both hands in front with the nondominant hand staying in front of the body as the "catching" hand. This becomes natural when your ready position has the nondominant hand on the racket.

Go to the ball; don't let the ball come to you. Keep your balance with your ready position in front, and be ready. To react, split step quickly with a wide base and your body behind your racket. By your playing the ball, you keep your balance, becoming a wall so that the ball seemingly bounces off the racket.

When the ball plays you, things become much different. Just reacting a little late puts you on the defensive, causing you to often step back away from the ball, taking you off-balance. The result is often a weak reply, creating an opportunity for your opponent to take the offensive and crush the next shot.

You can tell when either you play the ball or the ball plays you. See the ball off your opponent's racket and go to it; do not let it play you.

On slower shots, relax your fingers for more feel. Always "feel" the ball.

Staying balanced and volleying as if you are catching makes you seem like a wall, at least as it appears to your opponent. Don't miss. Be a wall. Set up before the ball gets there, staying balanced until it leaves. Maintaining balance puts pressure on your opponent by showing him that you are in control and that you won't miss. This pressure forces more errors from your opponent, forcing him to attempt lower-percentage shots with lower margins of error.

THE OVERHEAD

While the overhead is normally an offensive shot, most players try to do too much and often miss. Keep the overhead "smash" simple.

When you first realize you have an overhead, move to get underneath the ball. Once you're under the ball, get low. Most will actually initially try to move up to the ball too soon, prematurely straightening their legs, thus releasing and losing valuable stored kinetic energy. Fight the intuitive urge to move up to the ball; instead, get low. Once you're low, you're in a position to unload into the ball.

As the ball goes up, lower your center and turn sideways. As soon as possible get your head in line with the ball with your arms up, the racket hand by the ear, and the racket head to the inside of the handle. Keep the elbow up with the palm down. Like soccer, position your head in line with the ball as if you are going to head the ball. The ball should be coming down toward your forehead/hairline.

When making contact, feel as if you are hitting up, tapping the ball back into the sky. Most players wait too long to start their overhead swing. Try starting your swing when the ball is at its apex or when it just starts to drop. By starting early, you never rush, your arm is fully extended, and your energy is going up. Keep your fingers loose. Focus on extending your arm and racket up to the ball and making contact. If you can, time your contact with a wrist release, but don't muscle the ball. Too many mistakes come off mistimed "macho gorilla" shots intended to impress or intimidate. Win the point with smart, minimal-risk, offensive play. Save your attempts to impress for off-court activities.

When making contact, resist the "macho gorilla" urge to smash the ball. Treat the racket as a fly swatter rather than a club. Just make contact as if you were swatting a fly. Use a quick little snap, no more. Focus on contact rather than power, and your overheads will fare better.

THE DROP SHOT

Tennis teaching icon Dennis Van Der Meer is known to show the need for a loose racket on the drop shot with this demonstration. Place a racket on the ground with your foot on it, and drop a ball on the racket. Note how the ball bounces off the racket fairly firmly. Now do it again, but this time without your foot anchoring the racket. See how the ball almost dies on the racket! This is the drop shot.

When executing the drop shot, open the racket face. Relax the fingers and feel the ball on the racket. Let the ball "die" on the racket, almost as if the racket were lying on the ground unanchored.

In practicing the drop shot, see how many bounces you can get the ball to bounce inside the service box. Three bounces is usually a good drop shot. Keep feeling the ball on the racket until you can consistently drop the ball with at least three bounces in the service box. That's how to develop feel!

When hitting the drop shot, too many try to hit the ball close to and low over the net. Rather than go low over the net, think instead of setting your racket as if you were hitting a short lob. Yes, that's what we said, a lob. If your fingers are relaxed so that the ball "dies" on the racket, setting the racket as if for a short lob gives the drop shot the right trajectory and enough margin for error for a reliably effective stroke.

On faster balls, simply do less. Just point the racket tip to the net, relaxing the fingers to deaden the racket, allowing the ball to softly angle over the net.

Remember:
On the volley, move as if to catch the ball.
If you have time, move forward to the ball.
Be a wall.
Be there before the ball gets there, staying balanced until the ball leaves.

CHAPTER NINETEEN

THE SERVE

Grip—close to Continental. Many beginners learn to serve with the hammer grip that allows them to simply get the ball into play. Simply getting the ball into play does not work at the higher levels. The hammer grip blocks the wrist, limiting racket range of motion. The Continental grip or a grip closer to the Eastern backhand allows for greater motion through the ball, particularly when combined with pronation. Greater motion allows for greater acceleration that creates greater racket-head speed.

Elbow up at all times. Particularly with young players, check the elbow position. Some players drop the elbow; others raise their elbow. Getting the elbow parallel to the ground, as if throwing a baseball fastball, allows for a more complete kinetic chain from the shoulders through the arm and into the racket. Conversely, dropping or raising the elbow breaks the critical kinetic chain, limiting vitally important racket-head speed.

Racket face closed on take-back. Many players will open up the racket face too soon on the serve, thus creating more of a slingshot motion rather than an explosive snap up and through the ball. Keep the racket face closed with the palm down until the release.

Full arm extension on toss. Make sure the tossing arm extends fully through the toss, rather than simply launching the ball up. Full extension of the arm increases the chances of a rhythmic and full body extension drive up and into the ball. Full body extension allows for a better service angle over the net (thus effectively making the net shorter) and provides for a more complete kinetic chain of energy into the ball. The full arm extension also allows you to toss the ball a bit higher than you can reach, which further helps ensure your entire mass, not just your arm and racket, is driving up.

Weight transfer into court. Even at the beginner level, use the legs and body to push up through the ball and into the court. Players who are not used to this can start by simply stepping into the court with their back leg as they serve. In the modern game, players will drive up and into the ball, landing into the court with their front leg.

Shoulder over shoulder. Serving "shoulder over shoulder," like a cartwheel, is another critical parameter that helps optimize the kinetic chain of energy into the serve. Many players tend to toss too much to the right (or left for left-handers), which inhibits the ability to serve shoulder over shoulder.

Keeping the elbow up with the palm down is like throwing a fastball in baseball. The loading technique is the same. Serving in tennis is like throwing in baseball, except that one serves up in tennis, while often in baseball, one throws forward.

Often there is too much emphasis on loading the legs and snapping the wrist. Keep it simple. While making sure you have rhythm, once you load for the serve, let the legs and wrist take care of themselves. Let it happen. Keep the rhythm. Let the serve flow.

The serve is identical to throwing a racket in the sky. Look up! Lower, rotate, and release up. In your mind's eye, watch the racket flip head over tail up in the sky. If you threw two hundred rackets, you wouldn't let go at different places. Toss the ball to the spot where you would let go and then throw the racket up to and through the ball! Too many players look at their spot, look down at their opponent, and then serve! If you were to throw a racket over the fence, you would look over the fence, not at the fence; then you would tilt your spine, lower, load, rotate, and release up. By looking at the target service box or your opponent, your mind is down and your focus is down, which makes hitting and releasing up nearly impossible. Instead, envision an arc or rainbow in the path the ball will go. Your mind is where your eyes are. Look up when serving, rather than at your opponents.

Body turn takes the racket back.

Energy is focused *up*, with the hips moving slightly forward, tilting the spine angle.

Lower body naturally causes upper body lag, with the fingers staying loose at a level 3 tension.

Keep the head up; the body follows the head, so stay up! The shoulders dictate where the arm goes. Serve as if throwing the racket up, end over end.

Finish on balance.

Go down and up, not back and forth. This helps with the correct drive into the ball and gets the serve up and into the court.

Drive up with the quads. Keep the head up and drive with the legs. Keep the hips, not the head, over the baseline. Get the hips over the baseline and then drive up. If the head goes over the baseline before the hips, you can't help but fall forward and down; instead, you want to drive up into the ball. Also, to keep the head up more, hold the extended tossing arm just a split second longer.

Keep the grip and fingers loose. A loose grip and loose fingers help with relaxation, allowing for quicker racket acceleration. Then, release the racket up at contact as if you're cracking a whip *up* into the air.

When serving, think of throwing the racket through the ball. The serve is never a hit. "Hit" connotes effort with your mind tending to stop at rather than accelerating through the ball. Instead "throw" the racket up through the ball.

Another way to think of releasing the racket through the ball is to think of someone or something stopping your arm at impact. To demonstrate, move your arm through the air as if stroking and block the arm with the other arm. See how the wrist and hand continue forward when the arm is suddenly stopped. This is the release. Serve and think of someone blocking your arm at impact; do this, letting the hand and racket release and flow up through the ball.

This releasing, flowing action follows a natural law absolute, discussed earlier, that allows the body to create, accumulate, and transfer force during motion; one body part cannot accelerate forward until another body part stops. Here during the serve, tremendous energy is driven from the ground, accelerating through the legs, hips, core, shoulders, and arm; the feeling of releasing or blocking the arm continues to transfer that energy, accelerating *through* the wrist, hand, racket, and ultimately, the ball.

Service Spin

The way to master spin, whether slice or kick, is to commit and exaggerate. Whether kicking or slicing, commit to spin the ball and exaggerate the motion. For that matter, even when hitting the flat serve, exaggerate pronation by moving your thumb through the ball and out.

Focus staying in the present. Focus how you stroke through the ball instead of where it is going, which looks to the future. Focus on the present task of stroking the ball rather than the future result of where the ball may land.

Kick Serve

Feel as if the hand finishes along the baseline, not forward. In a sense, you want the feeling of the racket's path starting and finishing along the baseline. Accelerate the racket and let it rip out. Drive up, letting the racket go like a windshield wiper.

In hitting the kick serve, try to feel as many of the main strings as possible brush along the ball. Of course, to do this you have to feel the racket's path going more along the baseline, not forward.

Yet another way of thinking of the kick serve motion is of using the racket to roll a ball up a fence. Take a ball and, using a racket, hold it against a fence. Then use the racket to move the ball along the fence. Feel the racket move along the fence's plane, obviously without moving forward through the fence. The motion is very much like the optimal racket motion for the kick serve.

Remember:
When serving, envision the ball's path as an arc or rainbow.
Your mind is where your eyes are.
Look up as if you're throwing the racket at a cloud;
don't look at your opponent or target.
Throw your racket face "through" the ball;
don't "hit" the ball.
Toss a bit higher than you can reach to
ensure your entire mass goes up.

CHAPTER TWENTY

THE RETURN

The way to break one's will is to break his serve.

As we mentioned earlier, strength often becomes weakness because the ego invests in strength. Many players, especially power players, invest their ego in their serve. If you break their serve, you may break their ego and their will. The way to break a person's will, especially a power male, is to break his serve.

The return of serve is often an underappreciated and less-practiced shot. This defies common sense, considering that the return of serve is used by someone in 100 percent of all points played! While everyone practices his or her serve, not everyone treats the return with the same respect. Practice your return with the same diligence as your serve.

When returning serve, think first and foremost, "Turn the hips." It's not the shoulders; think instead, "Turn the hips." The upper body follows the lower body when relaxed!

Andre Agassi, one of the best returners of all time, is said to have said that the key to returning serve is turning the shoulders rather than thinking about swinging with the arms or moving the hands. It is dangerous territory to venture in to disagree with one of the best to have ever played the game, especially to dispute how to approach one of his signature shots.

First of all, on the return of serve, working with a player to either turn the shoulders or hips, as opposed to moving the arms, is good. Moving either the shoulders or hips provides a strong unit turn. Compared to someone making their initial move with the arms or hands, turning either the shoulders or hips improves the shot.

So while loading with the shoulders or hips is preferable to initially moving the arms or hands on the return, which is better when comparing solely the hips and the shoulders? We believe that loading and unloading with the hips is better.

By focusing on the hips rather than the shoulders, the laws of physics apply in providing for a stronger base and sequential rotation through the ball. When flowing, the upper body and shoulders follow the lower body and hips. Therefore, if the hips load and then unload, the shoulders will follow.

Unfortunately, the converse does not always ring true. Turning the shoulders first actually tends to reverse the natural sequential rotation and flow from the ground. In fact, one can actually turn or load the shoulders without turning the hips. By doing so, the sequential rotation for the return starts with the shoulders, losing much of the available ground force available through the legs and hips.

Widen your base. Keep the racket handle down. Load the hips, with your chest facing the ball, and turn into the ball. You don't even need to think of swinging your racket. Just load and turn the hips into the ball.

Always keep your perfect body position, just as you would if you were lifting weights. In keeping your buttocks low, think, "Sit down."

In readying for and actually returning serve, keep the following positions:
1. Keep the head still and balanced.
2. Keep the chin up.

3. Keep the shoulders level and perpendicular to the back.
4. Keep the buttocks low.
5. Keep a wide base to maximize a balanced power position.
6. Keep the back straight, as if it is a pole perpendicular to the ground.
7. Keep your chest facing the ball.

Keeping these positions all together provides a solid base and foundation, making the body much like a wall. By simply turning the hips and chest into the ball and taking the racket level through the ball, good things happen. Let your body be a wall. Be the wall.

When returning serve, think of catching the ball. Don't think of hitting. Instead, think of catching almost as if the racket were a baseball mitt. Move as if to catch the ball. Keep the attitude, "Can I catch the ball?" Then turn the hips into the ball. Keep the racket level through contact, aiming through the middle of the court. Keep the handshake position with the wrist through the shot; do not brush the ball.

In keeping your head level, think of your head as the bubble on a construction level tool. By leveling the level, you keep the bubble in the middle of the level tube. Keep your chin up. This helps a lot in stabilizing your head in the middle of the level. By keeping your head as the bubble in the middle of the imaginary level tool, you maintain balance.

In keeping your back straight, think of your back as an elevator shaft. If you need to lower your body, keep your back straight. If you need to go up, keep your back straight. When set, keep your back straight. Always keep your back straight. Keep the back straight and let the buttocks drop down, thus keeping your hips below you.

If you stop and lean forward, your knees will straighten, indicating a loss of balance. Rather, keep your hips low with your knees slightly flexed. Keep moving from the center of your body, even on the return.

Turn the hips, not the hands. In returning, many turn the hands as the reaction. If you first turn the hands and arm, the racket and racket face will turn and rotate naturally, as the radius bone rotates over the ulna, thus increasing the chance of losing control of the racket face. However, if you just turn the hips, the racket face can stay steady through the ball. Turning the hips facilitates stability and control; turning with the arm or hands loses control of the racket face and the shot.

Feel as if the body is a single unit, with the upper body feeling connected to the hips and legs. Keep the upper body more passive as the legs and hips do the work. Move with the sternum, trying to keep level balance through the shot and afterward.

In returning, aim through the center of the court. Think of hitting on a straight line all the way to the fence. If hitting through on a straight line, the ball should land close to the baseline almost every time. The key is in hitting straight through the ball with a wide base, staying balanced without lifting. Lift and the ball sails. Stay down and the ball should stay in. If the ball still goes long, close the racket face and take the racket more over the top of the ball on the next return.

One-Handed Backhand Return

Keep the handshake wrist angle with the racket head up and palm down, with the racket head slightly closed. Split step, move, load the hips, and contact as if catching the ball. Turn the hips through contact, keeping the racket head up with the handshake position. Think of hitting level to the back fence. The idea of hitting level to the back fence is a mind trick as it is impossible to do. If you hit the back fence, it is because you did not hit level. Think of hitting level to the back fence, and the lower body's natural rotation will produce natural topspin. Don't brush or lift. Just by rotating and coming around the outside of the ball, you'll create heavy pro spin, without brushing or lifting.

Remember:
When returning, move as if to "catch" the ball on balance.
Keep your back perpendicular to the ground
and your shoulders level.
Stay level and turn the hips.
Keep the racket face steady
with the palm down (racket face closed).

STROKE PARAMETER WORKSHEET	NOTES
NAME:	
FOREHAND	
Grip—between Eastern and semi-Western	
Unit turn	
Elbow away from body	
Racket head over hand on take-back	
Use of stances—open, semi-open, square	
Hands through ball	
Finish	
BACKHAND	
Grip—two-hand: bottom-hand Continental to Eastern	
Grip—two-hand: top-hand Eastern to semi-Western	
Grip—one hand: close to Eastern	
Unit turn	
Racket head over hand on take-back	
Tucking left elbow back, down, and through ball	
Use of stances—open, semi-open, square	
Hands through ball	
Finish	
VOLLEY	
Continental grip	
Ready position toward backhand side	
Limited backswing	
Slightly open racket face	
Feeling ball with hands	
SERVE	
Grip—close to Continental	
Elbow up at all times	
Racket face closed on take-back	
Full arm extension on toss	
Weight transfer into court	
Shoulder over shoulder	
RETURN OF SERVE	
Load with hips and shoulders	
Unload with hips rather than arms and hands	
Stable racket head through the ball with stable hands	
Stable and balanced head, chin up	

CHAPTER TWENTY-ONE

DOUBLES

When in doubt, work to set up your partner to put the ball away. Do what it takes to get your opponents off-balance so that they hit a ball your partner can win with. Often, doubles teams go for winners too soon. Patience is a virtue. Rather than look for the quick winner, look for the shot to set your partner up for the winner.

Server

The server's responsibility is to get 80 percent first serves in! Get the ball in play. Serve a majority of the serves at the body and up the tee. Change speed and spins.

Net Person

The net person's job is to get in the opposition's head. All too often, the server's partner or the receiver's partner remains passive, waiting for the ball to come to them. Passivity is wasted opportunity. Poach, fake, move. Do what it takes to be a factor.

On *every* serve that goes by your head, move forward toward the net. As your opponent starts his swing, either fake to poach by moving your racket toward the center of the court and stepping that way, or actually *poaching*! As the opponent starts his swing, move diagonally to the net strap. Don't time it. Get there as fast as you can, with your shoulders facing the ball, not to where you are moving. If you stay low, the net protects you from the waist down. Keep your hands up.

Be a factor, not a sniper. No one sees a sniper because he doesn't move! The net person's job is to be seen, felt, and avoided. Keep moving whether poaching or not.

Returner

Set up, lower the hips, and turn. "Catch" the ball and rotate hips into the ball. Keep the shoulders level and back straight.

Returning Partner

There are three positions for the returner's partner, depending on the strength of the players involved and the situation.

1. Defensive—when you're not getting in the point or you're a target at the net and you're not winning a high-enough percentage of points. Stand just inside the baseline looking for any short balls.
2. Neutral position—this is the traditional position for the receiver's partner. Stand at the service line facing the net person, covering more of the center of the court. If the return goes to the net person, dig in, press forward, and challenge him. You're in the hot seat. If the return goes back to the server, move forward and challenge his first volley. Fake a poach or actually poach. It is your responsibility to be a threat and a playmaker. You are closest to the net. The closer you get to the net, the better angles you have and the less time your opponents have!
3. Offensive—when you have supreme confidence in your partner's return. Start closer to net and look for every opportunity to move to the ball after your partner's return. Be a factor. Be a force at the net.

Remember, when you are at the baseline, your angles of coverage to your opponents' court are 20 degrees. From the middle of the service box, you have 30 degrees; three feet from the net, you have 120 degrees! The closer you are to the net, geometrically the more court you have to hit into, while you also take time away from your opponents. When you're three feet from the net, as opposed to the baseline, your opponents have half the time and six times the court to cover! Make life easier for you and your partner; get to net!

CHAPTER TWENTY-TWO

DRILLS

Warming up. When warming up, start up closer to the net, preferably hitting soft shots in the service boxes. Stay controlled, feeling your hands and racket on the ball and feeling your feet on the court. Even in warm-up, move your feet. All too often people warm up with short-court tennis, stroking the ball back and forth without moving their feet. Inevitably, misses occur.

Don't do this. Instead, feel the ball with your hands and the court with your feet. *Warm up!* As you feel and groove more and more, gradually move back so that after a minute or so, you are hitting from the baseline. Keep the ball in play; don't miss. Too often in warming up, players move back to the baseline where they pound the ball back and forth in almost mock battle. This is not the time for battle or winners; this is the time for warm-up.

Pressure and repetition in practice drills. No matter what the shot, whether with a live ball or from a fed ball setting, a goal of stroking a particular number in provides more purposeful practice by giving pressure while honing strokes. Set a goal and work to meet the goal without excuse or softening. For instance, hand-feed one hundred forehands without a miss. If the player misses, start again. This works for forehands, backhands, and other strokes, as well as hand and racket feeds and live-ball stroking.

Hopman drill (volley). In honor of legendary Australian coach Harry Hopman, this drill focuses on volleying *through* the ball. Players volley to each other from the service line, trying to hit through the baseline. By exaggerating just a little, this drill teaches depth and more solid volleying.

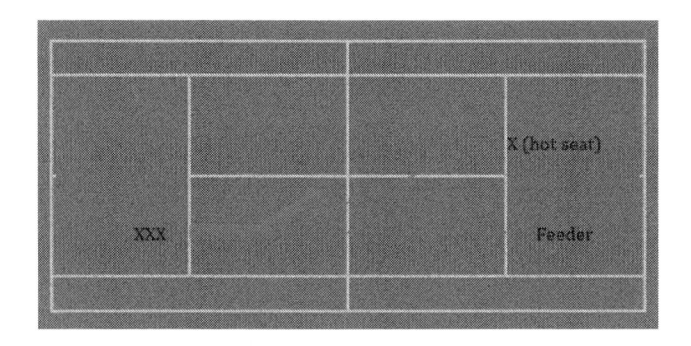

HOT-SEAT-APPROACH DRILL

Pro feeds to line. First person in line hits to hot seat and closes, playing out the point. Continue the same with the second person in line and so forth.

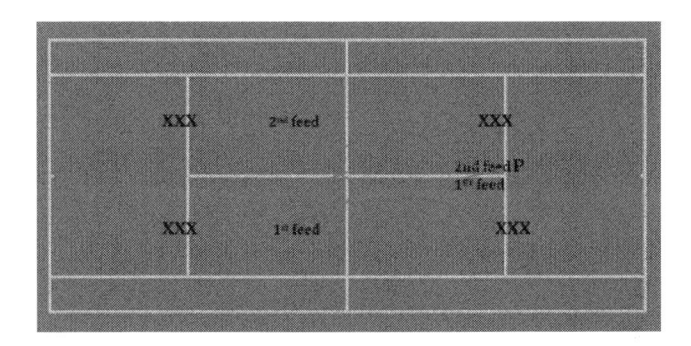

DOUBLES DIAGONAL DRILL

Pro feeds to the first person in one line, who volleys crosscourt to the first person in the opposing line. They play out the point. Pro then feeds to the first person in the alternate line, who volleys crosscourt to his opposite, playing out the point. Players move to the back of the line after each point they play.

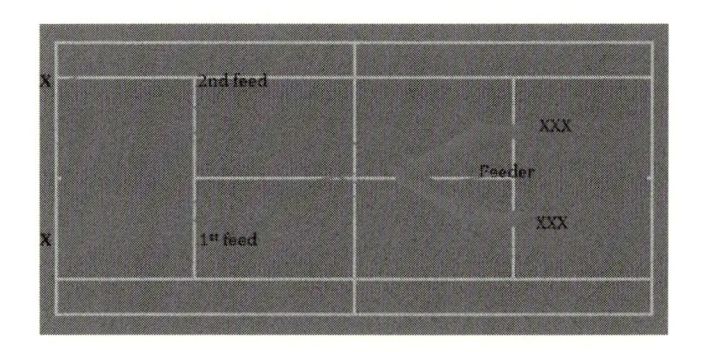

RETURN FROM THE AIR / DIAGONAL VOLLEY POACHING DRILL

Pro feeds ball *through* the baseline so that returner has to stroke/return from the air through the middle. First person in line diagonal from the returner poaches, cutting across to cut off the return. Poacher then goes to the back of the other line, while pro feeds second ball *through* the baseline to the other side with the drill repeating.

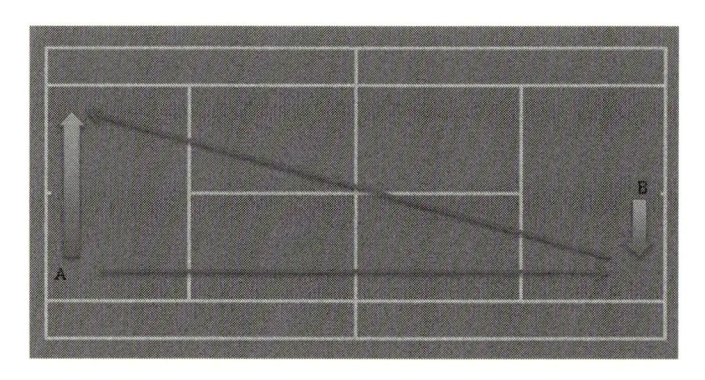

CROSSCOURT OPEN-COURT DRILL

Player A, who is positioned to the side of the court, feeds down the line to player B, initially positioned at center court. Player B hits crosscourt to the open court, and the players play out the point.

Approach-volley drill (transition, volleys, doubles). Players start with a feed at three-fourth court and then move to net for volleys and finishing play. Drill both with crosscourt, down the line, and through the middle feeds. The drill works with two or four players.

Approach-shot drill. Feeder/player starts on deuce side and feeds ball short to opponent. May feed high or low, but not deep or wide; if the feed is too deep or too wide, refeed the ball. Players play the point to win. Play points on either side. Play games to seven or eleven points. To take the drill to the next level, the feeder/player starts in the middle and moves over to the forehand or backhand side to set up for the fastball.

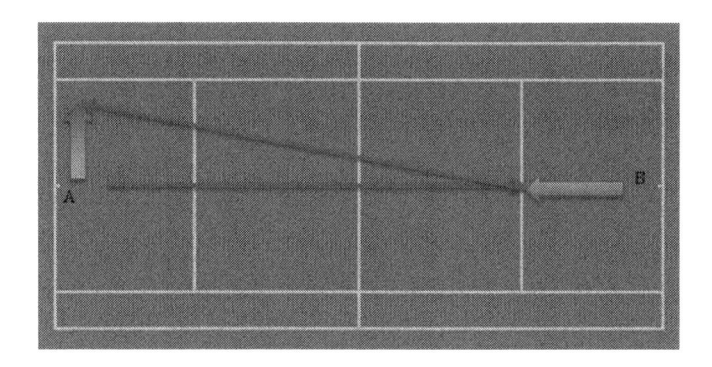

APPROACH-SHOT DRILL

Player A feeds short midcourt ball to player B, who is inside, at, or behind the baseline. Player B moves in to approach to one corner. Players play out the point. Vary drill by going first to one corner, then to another, and through midcourt.

Kick serve drill. Stand close to the back baseline fence and spin the ball up over the back from close to the fence.

Kick serve drill. Exaggeration is the way to master spin. Try to kick the ball as high over the net as possible—and we mean as high as possible. Try to hit the serve twenty feet up into the air with enough spin so that it still goes in. Once you learn to do this, hitting the "normal" spin serve seems so much easier.

Flat serve drill. Serve from half court and see how high up on the fence you can serve the ball from serving in the box. Ultimate success is to serve the ball into the service box to bounce over the back fence (a feat that very, very few can achieve).

Short-angle and one-hand backhand drill. A drill for decreasing the radius of the arm to increase racket-head speed. Reach across and grab your triceps with your nondominant hand. Then shadow-stroke with the elbow rotating. This is a good exercise for the one-handed backhand and for tight-angle shots on both the forehand and backhand.

Second-serve-only drill. Play points, games, and sets with only second serves. This develops a more effective second serve by creating pressure-match-type situations.

Twenty overhead drill. Hit twenty consecutive overheads in. If you miss, start over. One variation is to mix in volleys with the overheads. If you miss a volley, subtract one from the overhead total. As with the basic drill, if you miss an overhead, start over.

Twenty volley drill. Hit twenty consecutive volleys in. If you miss, start over.

Seven service drill. Hit seven consecutive slice serves in. If you miss, start over. Then hit seven consecutive kick serves in, also starting over if you miss. Finish with seven consecutive flat serves in. You can also practice locational serving by dividing the service box into halves or thirds, depending on how precisely you want to serve. Once you master seven consecutive serves, go to ten or whatever number is achievable. Former German professional player Alexander Waske once hit twenty-eight flat serves in consecutively! Get in the flow, focus on your serve, and you may surprise yourself how many you can hit in!

Van Drillen. Named after former pro player Erik van Dillen, the Van Drillen drill combines aggressive net play and volleying with passing shots and powerful ground stroking. The drill starts with one person at midcourt and one at the baseline. The midcourt player feeds the ball to the baseliner, immediately closing on the net, looking to volley and win the point. The ground stroker attempts to pass or lob and win the point. The volleyer cannot let the ground stroker's reply hit the ground. If the ball hits the ground on the midcourt/volleyer's side, the ground stroker wins two points. Conversely, by hitting a clean winner, the midcourt/volleyer wins two points. Otherwise, each point won counts as one.

Sometimes, play the Van Drillen on half the court up and down the line to take away crosscourt passing angles. This variation makes clean winners more difficult for both players and encourages greater shot tolerance.

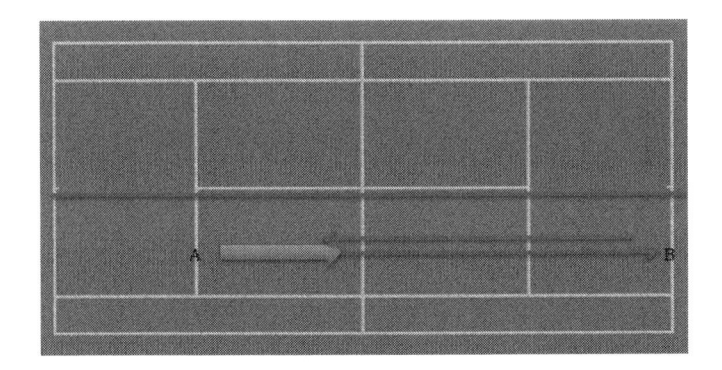

VAN DRILLEN

The drill starts with players A at midcourt and B at the baseline. Player A feeds the ball to B and closes on the net, looking to volley and win the point. Player B attempts to pass or lob and win the point. Player A cannot let B's replies hit the ground. If the ball hits the ground on A's side, player B wins two points. Conversely, by hitting a clean winner, player A wins two points. Otherwise, each point won counts as one.

ATP singles drill. This is a good format for practicing singles play with three players, two on one side of the net and one on the other. One way is for the sole player to return and play simultaneous separate games against the other two players. The other two players serve, each alternating by serving two points and each keeping separate score against the returner. Once a server holds serve by winning a complete game, he changes places with the returner, and all three start over. If the returner breaks one server's service game, the other server continues with his current game. This drill provides ongoing play with pressure in different score situations and a focus on performing.

Another variation is to reverse the format so that the sole player serves with the other two players returning.

Plus-minus drill. A competitive drill that simulates a potentially extended game situation, promoting concentration and intensity. Players play points, keeping score until either one player is ahead by a preagreed margin, such as "plus 5" points or "minus 5" points. A normally scored game involves just a two-point margin; competing with a larger victory margin promotes sustained concentration. Play either with serves or initial hand feeds for ground-stroke games.

Yup drill. Renamed from the bounce/hit drill for tennis student Laura Martin because calling out "yup" is easier than calling out "bounce" or "hit," this drill develops perception, reaction, and setting up skills. Call out "yup" when the ball is on the opponent's racket, and work to split step by the time you call "yup." Additionally, call out "yup" when the ball bounces on your side of the court, and work to set up by the time the ball bounces.

This drill heightens awareness of hard focus and motivates to split step and set up earlier.

Feeding Drills

Side to side. Any quantity. Down the line, crosscourt, and angles. Emphasize proper footwork depending on the feed and the court position, whether stepping into the ball on offensive shots or hitting with open stance on wide or deep balls.

Side to side with restrictions. Examples of restrictions can be hitting deep, hitting with specific spin, or hitting a specific shot. Other examples are hitting offensively, defensively, or neutralizing, all of which need perfecting.

Four-ball drill. From a fed ball, with either a forehand or backhand, hit four shots with exactly the same setup and rhythm: down the line, crosscourt, short angle, and lob. The player should always set up as if going down the line. This drill develops "holding" and feel while emphasizing the highest level of footwork.

Six-ball drill. The same drill as the four ball drill, but also add inside-out and inside-in shots.

Eight-ball drill. Similar to the four-ball drill but alternating between forehand and backhand for the same progression: down the line (forehand and backhand), crosscourt (forehand and backhand), short angle (forehand and backhand), and lob (forehand and backhand). Maintain the same setup and rhythm for each shot.

All forehands, down the line, and inside out. Player starts in the middle with the first feed toward the sideline, which he hits down the line. The second feed is back to the middle of the court to which the player must recover and drive an inside-out forehand. Do any number of repetitions, up to thirty.

Three-ball forehand. Feed a forehand down the line, then a forehand inside out, finishing with a forehand inside in. Feed to three separate spots. Do five sets of three balls. One variation is to finish the third ball with a backhand rather than an inside-in forehand. Make sure the player is specific on each and every shot.

Forehands or backhands to one side. Player hits a specified number of forehands or backhands to one area of the court. Emphasize recovery after the shot and intensity on executing each stroke.

Sidestep or cross-step drill. Player starts on doubles sideline, side-or cross steps to the middle, and is then fed a wide ball to the other side to which he turns and runs to stroke. Player hits crosscourt or down the line and then must recover to the middle with side-or cross steps, and then moves to the opposite side to stroke. This drill strengthens footwork, improves setup and anticipation, as well as making the player learn to face the court.

Spanish drill. Coach feeds short ball and then deep ball. Teaches moving forward and backward. Quantity is dependent on coach.

X-drill. A variation on the Spanish drill, where the player is fed a pattern of four balls starting with a short forehand, then a deep forehand, followed by a short backhand and deep backhand to complete the first *X*. From the first deep backhand, feed continuously to the short forehand to start the next *X*. Do three sets of four balls for a total of twelve each turn.

Defense drill. Coach feeds high and deep with excessive topspin, moving the player back and side to side. Player must learn to step back and, aggressively off the back foot, hit a heavy defensive ball. Player must recover to the baseline to emphasize forward and back footwork.

Typewriter drill. Player starts on doubles line and is fed multiple balls along the baseline toward the opposite doubles line, and then back to the starting position. Player should receive at least four forehand and four backhands in each full sequence. Set up targets for more specificity.

Multiple-player drills, two-ball drills. The variations are almost endless for multiple line players, even with only two balls per turn. Try the following:

- Backhand cross and forehand on the run
- Forehand cross and backhand on the run
- Forehand on the run with short backhand approach
- Forehand on the run with drop shot feed to which player must reply with redrop shot
- Opposite sides with variations

Chair drill (volley). Place a chair on the court in the service box where players normally volley. With the player sitting in the chair, first feed balls at waist height to him, which he catches without a racket. Then feed balls to him, which he volleys with a racket as if he is catching the ball. He should just be an athlete, not worrying about the stroke. By sitting in the chair, the player keeps his back straight and shoulders level. In catching the ball, the player keeps his hands in front rather than moving them to the side or behind.

This drill helps to simplify the volley. Volleying is like catching. While most people catch naturally and efficiently, they also tend to complicate matters when volleying. Catching teaches and reinforces the natural and biomechanically correct way to volley.

Return-from-the-air drill (return). The player stands in the return position. From the service tee on the other side, the feeder feeds line drive waist-height balls in the air through the baseline. Moving as if to catch the ball, the player turns through the ball in the air, ideally redirecting the ball back through the middle of the court. In turning through the ball, the player should focus on keeping the back straight and shoulders level. One common mistake is tilting the shoulders, which causes a loss of balance. Keep the shoulders level. Stroke by first loading and then unloading the hips through the ball. Emphasize the hips, not the hands or the shoulders.

Approach shots. Player starts on baseline and is fed simple short balls. Emphasize discipline in setting up with balance before stroking the ball. Always set up as if hitting down the line.

Cone drill. Set up a cone two feet behind the center baseline. Player hits forehand or backhand, then recovering by sidestepping and backpedaling in front and around the cone, then moving for the next ball. This emphasizes player movement and recovery. Put body weight into each shot. Each shot should look as if the player is following the ball to net, even if the shot is open stance.

Scrambling drill. Player is fed multiple balls around the court. The coach is responsible for making the feeds realistic. For example, grinding out a point, or transition balls after long side-to-side exchanges, pushing balls behind the players, etc.

Home base drill with three to five balls. Player starts at home base, around the center baseline. First ball is deep, defensive ball, after which player recovers to home base. Second ball is normal, basic rally ball, after which player recovers home. Third ball is transition or attack ball, followed by volley and overhead. Use whatever sequence gets the most out of the player.

Serve and feed drill. Player serves a first or second serve. Coach then feeds return. Fed ball can be rally, short, or volley, depending on what style the player is practicing.

Catching drill with no racket. Without a racket, player should set up just like a ground stroke and catch the ball. This is basic but instrumental in teaching a balanced foundation and contact point. Also important for approach shots and volleys. Stroking is like catching; if you can get to the ball to catch, you can get to the ball to stroke. Furthermore, if you can get your strings on the ball as if catching, you can put the ball in play into the court.

Fastball drill. Player is on the baseline. Coach feeds extremely fast ball close to the baseline, forcing the player to react. This practices neutralizing and countering balls crushed at the player. Important keys are keeping the back straight, butt down as if sitting, and making a good, strong, quick turn. Take a short backswing, staying down, and turn through the ball, following through around the waist.

Inside baseline drill. Player takes fed balls inside the baseline with any side-to-side variation. Player should focus on taking balls early, working the legs, and set up.

CHAPTER TWENTY-THREE

PHYSICAL FITNESS AND TRAINING

If you are not physically fit, you cannot function to your maximum potential. Use a physical fitness program to improve coordination, endurance, equilibrium, flexibility, strength, and speed. In today's modern game, simply playing tennis, unfortunately, is not enough. To fulfill your potential and maximize performance, you must do more than play and hit tennis balls.

Reaction ball. Using a Z-ball or multisided reaction ball helps develop hard focus, anticipation, and reaction speed. By yourself or with a partner, toss the ball and catch after the bounce. The uncertain and relatively unpredictable bounce forces you to time your split step on the bounce, as much as you need to time your split step to the ball off your opponent's racket.

Ladder. A flexible plastic or cloth ladder is a great tool for footwork agility and speed. While the number of possibilities abound, the core footwork drills consist of the following:

- *Forward run, single rung.* Run straight through with one step in each ladder's rung. Work on speed, keeping the feet in contact with the ground for as little time as possible.
- *Forward run, double rung.* Run straight through but through every other rung. This exercise allows for longer, evenly spaced steps.
- *Sidestep, single rung.* Move through the ladder sideways with each foot stepping in each rung. Work on quickness and balance, keeping each foot on the ground for as little time as possible. Move in one direction with the right foot leading, then repeat with the left foot leading.

- *Sidestep, double rung.* Move as with the sidestep, single rung, except that lengthen the stride so that the lead foot steps in every other rung with the adjacent foot stepping in each adjacent rung so that the feet step in separate rungs. Move in one direction with the right foot leading, then repeat with the left foot leading.
- *Ickey shuffle.* Named for former Cincinnati Bengal football player Ickey Woods, this drill uses his celebratory touchdown dance shuffle for agility and speed. Start with the left foot to the side. Shuffle both feet into the first rung with just the right foot moving out to the right side. Then the left foot moves up one rung, followed by the right foot moving back into the ladder on the same rung. The left foot moves back out to the side, while the right foot moves up to the third rung. Keep the sequence going through the whole ladder. With experience and feel, the sequence goes faster and faster with a developing quickness and rhythm, much like dancing.

Tennis soccer. A fun drill that combines soccer, tennis, and volleyball to develop balance, agility, and footwork. With a soccer ball and either two or four players, use the feet, head, and body, but not the hands or arms, to kick or hit the ball over the net into the service boxes. Start by "serving" by kicking the ball from behind the service line over the net and into the other service boxes. The ball may bounce twice on each side before the players must return. The typical point consists of the player "receiving" serve by letting the serve bounce, trapping the ball with the chest, letting it bounce once more, and then either kicking or heading the ball back into the other court. Play games up to an agreed number, such as seven points to win.

Medicine ball throws. Medicine ball throws help develop explosive power through the core and legs while mimicking both forehand and backhand motions. With two hands, load to the side and then unload the hips and core, throwing the ball forward. Do on both forehand and backhand sides. Also do overhand throws with the medicine ball, making sure that you launch the ball primarily up, rather than forward. There is some forward motion, but make sure the primary motion is up.

Medicine ball mini-tennis. Similar to tennis soccer, use medicine balls to throw back and forth into the service boxes. This drill requires medicine balls that bounce. Throw using the forehand or backhand motion. Players throw back and forth, trying to win the point as in tennis, with no more than one bounce in each court. Play games up to an agreed number, such as seven points to win.

Bands. Now a staple of most professional players, resistance bands develop flexibility and strength, especially in the arms and shoulders. The following exercises set forth some basic routines. All presume starting and carrying the motion through resistance, so start each motion with the band sufficiently anchored so that the band resists the required motion.
- *External rotation.* Standing holding the resistance band with the elbow cocked at ninety degrees, the lower arm at a right angle and parallel to the ground, rotate the arm away from the body with resistance.
- *Internal rotation.* Standing holding the resistance band with the elbow cocked at ninety degrees and the lower arm parallel to the ground, rotate the arm into the body with resistance.
- *Push-downs.* Standing holding the resistance band with the elbow cocked at ninety degrees and the hand at head level, the lower arm straight to the side of the body but perpendicular to the ground, push the lower arm down so that it is parallel to the ground with the hand at shoulder level. Hold the upper arm steady

in a straight line through the shoulders so that the shoulder does all the work in pushing the resistance band down.
- *Pull-ups.* Reverse of the push-downs, start with the lower arm straight by shoulder and down parallel to the ground. Raise the arm up so that it finishes perpendicular to the ground and at head level.
- *Standing rows.* With resistance, pull the bands with one or two hands toward the body at chest level.

Running. Tennis is a wonderful combination of aerobic and anaerobic activity. The complete tennis athlete needs stamina, endurance, power, and speed. Both sprinting and reasonable long distance runs help to develop and complement a player's needs.

- Long distance runs help develop the aerobic system and, while not directly helping in the short bursts of energy required for tennis points, assist in developing stamina and minimizing recovery times between points. Run continuously from fifteen minutes to longer, depending on what is manageable.

- Sprinting helps develop anaerobic capacity and speed. Run laps around the court, sprinting along the sidelines, broken by jogging along the baseline. To practice shorter bursts of speed, run laps by sprinting full speed along the baseline, broken by jogging along the sidelines.

Jumping rope. Skipping rope helps develop stamina, endurance, footwork, and balance. In addition to normal jump roping, try jumping rope slowly but with jumping three fast steps with each slow rope revolution. This hyperjumping overloads the body, conditioning the body, feet, and mind to work faster.

Alignment rods. Alignment rods are often used by golfers to monitor balance and connectedness. Tennis players can also learn from alignment rods to develop a better sense of balance and the kinetic chain. Use two rods, connecting one to the shoulders and the other to the hips. Keep in mind that the shoulders follow the hips, and the arms follow the shoulders. Turn the hips first and feel the shoulders follow with the arms following the shoulders.

CONCLUSION

Martial arts carries as integral components time-honored principles of personal mastery and athletic performance. Tennis, the sport for a lifetime, has much to learn from accepting and adhering to basic martial arts fundamentals—not only physically and technically, but also personally, emotionally, and psychologically. Examining martial arts sheds light on common denominators of athletic performance, which transfer and apply to every sport.

This book sets forth a number of fundamentals for athletic performance, most specifically tennis. While in the West many of these fundamentals are ignored, especially the intangible nonphysical, an athlete cannot fulfill his potential without focusing on the full panoply of fundamentals, physically tangible *and* the psychologically and emotionally intangible. Becoming a complete competitor and tennis master requires completely committing to each and every fundamental, including those that improve attitude and learning skills.

Mastering each fundamental represents a journey into improvement and excellence not only for tennis and martial arts as specific disciplines but also for overall personal fulfillment and mastery in life.

Embrace a learning mind-set for everything. Look for the opportunity to learn from *everything.* Learn purposefully and with discipline. Relentlessly persevere in whatever you do, including learning, practice, and competing. Develop confidence through practice and experience.

Stay in the present and focus on what is happening *now.* Lose yourself in the process. Dispense with your ego in the moment; go with the flow, fearing nothing. Stay calm and relaxed, as the moment really is the only thing. Feel ying and yang, flow and force. Breathe fully as you relax in the present, without self, without fear, with the mind and body as one, making everything simple.

Be ready. Look to the greatest threat. Move from the ground, staying balanced.

Set up and use earth's power to stroke from the ground, driving and rotating through the legs, hips, core, shoulders, arm, and racket. Strike through the ball and follow through. Stay simple. Stay smart.

Mastering these fundamentals unlocks the power of action, unleashing the fulfilling power of self. Paradoxically, dispensing with the self's ego leads one to self-actualization and fulfillment. Learn and master these fundamentals and you'll not only become a much better tennis player; you'll also become a better learner, performer, and athlete. Much, much more importantly, you'll become a better person.

ACKNOWLEDGMENTS

First and foremost, I must thank Coach John Nelson for agreeing to work with me on this project and share his personal wealth of knowledge in tennis and martial arts. From the first time I heard John speak, I was impressed and motivated by his common sense yet innovative approach and perspective. John's passion and integrity made this project truly fulfilling. Writing a book is an intensive process, and John has been a welcomed partner and companion in this journey to help others master the wonderful sport of tennis.

A special thanks goes to graphic designer and friend Doug Char, who designed the cover and illustrated the inside cover. Also thanks to fellow coach Joël Kusnierz for providing his tennis technique and modeling skills in posing for the book's instructional photos.

I also thank those who have helped and mentored me throughout my tennis career including but not limited to Chan Bearce, Sam Caldwell, Gavin Hopper, Rick Leipold, Dave Porter, and Henry Talbert. Each of these individuals has enlightened not only my life but also the tennis world in his own special way.

Mark A. Beede

The writing of this book has been a journey like my growth as a Christian and as a coach. I have had many quality people in my life who have influenced my outlook and my approach to coaching. I want to acknowledge them here, as this book would not have been possible without them.

First, I would like to thank God for all blessings come from him. I have been blessed with finding my passion and making a living at it for thirty-eight years.

My wife, Carol, for thirty-two years of marriage has loved me and let me pursue my goals. Without her support, it would not have been possible.

My parents, Ray and Ruby Nelson, allowed my twin brother (Jeff) and me to compete in many sports, from baseball, wrestling, and soccer to martial arts and, finally, tennis. They made many sacrifices for our family for which I am thankful.

Having a twin brother, one learns to compete and strive in everything he does. Thanks, Jeff. Thank you to my brother Jim Nelson, a policeman who always had the courage to stand up for what is right.

Thanks also to Jack Henn, former San Diego State volleyball coach, and Mike Sanchez, former Mesa College baseball coach, for their friendship, support, and technical insight into their respective sports.

Rich Anderson, my Canada College tennis coach, developed his teams as an educator, expecting us to get good grades. He developed his players mentally, physically, and technically.

Dick Gould, Stanford University tennis coach. Dick's professionalism and program development set, and continue to set, the bar for all coaches in any sport. Dick had a vision and a goal and was committed to it. His teams dominated college tennis for over two decades, when he garnered the honor of NCAA Division 1 Coach of the Decade—not once, but twice. Yet, even with his success, Dick always remained personable, respectful, and humble.

My sensei Sig Kufferath taught hand-to-hand combat in the US Army in 1944 in Honolulu. Of German and Japanese descent, Sig grew up in Hawaii during WWII, experiencing racism and hatred. He always remained calm, loving, and giving of himself. Entrusted with teaching the art of Kodenkan Danzan Ryu jujitsu, Sig taught the discipline, mastery of techniques, respect for authority and others, the never-ending pursuit of knowledge, and how to face and overcome fear. He made me realize that most limitations are self-imposed.

My sensei Richard Bunch always spoke of jujitsu as the art of winning. Rich always stressed the preparation for real life, teaching street fighting and survival situations as compared to just sport fighting. He taught us to fight with our strengths against our opponents' weaknesses, knowing that your mind is your best weapon.

My friend Bob Vocker, a golf professional, has spent many years with me sharing insights about the similarities of golf and tennis—from the technical and mental to applied physics.

Denny Dickenson has been my friend and mentor for twenty-five years. Denny, who has his doctorate in psychology from Stanford University, has given freely of his time and expertise to help me and my tennis programs, serving also as a major booster for my programs.

Joël Kusnierz, my assistant coach for his friendship and sharing his insights to my philosophy to teaching and coaching. We have spent many hours on and off the court discussing my approach.

For many years people have asked me to put a lot of these principles in a book. I want to thank Mark Beede, who has spent almost two years of watching my tennis lessons most mornings and my afternoon team practices. He questioned and challenged me as to what and why I'm teaching the specific principles I teach. He has been instrumental in the writing of this book.

And finally I would like to thank all of the players I have coached over the years. I have learned from all of you. *Mahalo!*

John Nelson

REFERENCES

Beckett, Samuel. 1983. *Worstward Ho.* New York: Grove Press.

Beede, Mark A. 2016. *From Go to Pro—a Playing and Coaching Manual for the Aspiring Tennis Player (and Parents): Developing the Elite Tennis Player.* Indianapolis, IN: Xlibris.

Compact Oxford English Dictionary. 2005. Oxford: Oxford University Press

Diaz, Jaime. 2002. "Tiger Woods v. Jack Nicklaus." http://golfdigest.com/story/diaz_tigervsjack)_gd0211.

Dweck, Carol S. 2006. *Mindset: The New Psychology of Success.* New York, NY: Ballantine Books.

Elderton, Wayne. 2010. "Learning Tennis as an Open Skill." *Coach to Coach Newsletter.* AceCoach.com.

Elliott, Bruce, Reid Machar, and Crespo Miguel. 2009. *Technique Development in Tennis Stroke Production.* London: International Tennis Federation.

Forbes, Gordon. 1978. *A Handful of Summers.* New York: Lyons & Burford.

Gallwey, W. Timothy. 1974. *The Inner Game of Tennis: The Classic Guide to the Mental Side of Peak Performance.* New York: Random House.

Hess, Joseph C. 1982. *Night Stick.* Burbank, CA: Ohara Publications.

Kiegiel, Ted. 1999. *Balanced Golf: Harnessing the Simplicity, Focus, and Natural Motions of Martial Arts to Improve Your All-Around Game.* Chicago, IL: Contemporary Books.

Koga, Robert, and John G. Nelson. 1967. *The Koga Method: Police Weaponless and Defense Techniques.* Beverly Hills, CA: Glencoe Press.

LaSanta, David. "Buster Douglas v Mike Tyson (Motivational)." Online video clip, YouTube. Posted March 22, 2016. Viewed March 23, 2016.

Lee, Bruce. 2016. *Striking Thoughts: Bruce Lee's Wisdom for Daily Living.* Edited by John Little. North Clarendon, VT: Tuttle Publishing.

Loehr, James E. 1982. *Mental Toughness Training for Sports: Achieving Athletic Excellence.* Lexington, MA: The Stephen Greene Press.

Malaska, Mike. 2013. *I Feel Your Pain: Let's Make Golf Uncomplicated.* St. Louis, MO: Nies.

Maltz, Maxwell. 1960. *Psycho-Cybernetics.* New York: Simon & Schuster.

Murray, John. 1999. *Smart Tennis: How to Play and Win the Mental Game.* San Francisco: Jossey-Bass Publishers.

Psychology Solution Shining New Light on Old Problems. 2016. "Secrets of Confident People." www.psychology-solution.com/confidence/confident-people. Posted December 14, 2016. Viewed December 13, 2016.

Richardson, Alan. 1967. "Mental Practice: A Review and Discussion" (Parts 1 and 2). *Research Quarterly* 38, no. 1. American Association for Health, Physical Education and Recreation.

Robson, Tim. 2003. *The Hitting Edge: How to Excel at the Plate*. Champaign, IL: Human Kinetics.

Serbian Journal of Sport Science. 2011. "The Effects of Vision Training on Performance in Tennis Players."

Syed, Matthew. 2010. *Bounce: The Myth of Talent and the Power of Practice*. London: Fourth Estate.

Toole, F. X. 2000. *Rope Burns: Stories from the Corner.* New York: Ecco Press.

Trick Shot Tennis. 2014. "Insane Volley Drill!!!! Cara Black Trick Shot Tennis." Online video clip, YouTube. Posted September 1, 2014. Viewed January 30, 2016.

Wallace, David Foster. 2016. *String Theory: David Foster Wallace on Tennis.* New York: Little, Brown & Co.

Williams, Mark A., Paul Ward, Nicholas J. Smeeton, and David Allen. 2004. "Developing Anticipation Skills in Tennis Using On-Court Instruction: Perception versus Perception and Action." *Journal of Applied Sport Psychology* 16:350–60.

Yellin, Steve, and Buddy Biancalana. 2010. *The 7 Secrets of World Class Athletes*. Lexington, KY: PMPM Sports.

ABOUT THE AUTHORS

John Nelson

John Nelson has been at the helm of the University of Hawaii men's tennis team since the 2003–04 season. After years of building the program with top-flight recruits and instilling a winning attitude in his players, the program has reaped the benefits with multiple conference titles and NCAA tournament appearances.

Nelson takes pride in player development. He works to develop his players mentally, physically, and technically, nurturing their development and challenging them with the best competition the nation has to offer.

Prior to the University of Hawaii, Nelson served as head coach at San Diego State for ten years, at UC Davis for five years, and at Cal State Hayward for six years. At San Diego State, he guided the team to multiple NCAA tournament appearances and earned several ITA Regional Coach of the Year awards, as well as the Mountain West Coach of the Year honor in 2002.

Also at San Diego State, he coached Alexander Waske, who went on to the tour, earning wins over world top-ranked players Rafael Nadal and the Bryan brothers. At UC Davis, Nelson's team won the NCAA Division II team title in 1992. During his UC Davis tenure, one singles players and three doubles teams won individual national championships. At Cal State Hayward, without any athletic scholarships, his Pioneers ranked in the nation's top 10 in each year, while John earned eight conference and four regional Coach of the Year awards and the 1992 NCAA Division II National Coach of the Year honor.

At each of these schools, Nelson coached either a singles or doubles individual NCAA champion, along with eight Division I and twenty-two Division II All-Americans. At four different universities, Nelson's teams have won nineteen conference championships in thirty-five years at the NCAA level.

As a player, Nelson played at Canada College in Redwood City, California, where he earned an associate of arts degree in physical education. He later went on to become an NCAA Division II All-American at Cal State Hayward, where in 1978 he earned a bachelor's of science degree in kinesiology and physical education that same year. During his years at CSUH, Nelson was named to the NCAA All-Star team that played Mexico in Mexico City.

In 1979, Nelson earned a master's degree in education from Stanford University.

Professionally, Nelson has played tennis in Europe and in Northern California, where he was ranked sixth in doubles with his twin brother, Jeff.

He is a member of the USPTA and formerly served on the board of directors for the Intercollegiate Tennis Association.

Nelson is a third-degree black belt in jujitsu and has studied judo, aikido, kali, shotokan karate, and taekwondo and uses martial art skills in tennis. Nelson resides in Honolulu with his wife, Carol.

Mark A. Beede

Mark Beede is a USPTA-, PTR-, and ATPCA-certified tennis coach, manager, and educator. Born and raised in Maine, USA, Beede received his undergraduate degree from Brandeis University and law degree from the University of Maine School of Law. After practicing law for sixteen years, Mark changed careers to tennis and moved to Hawaii to work with the USTA–Hawaii Pacific section and the Hawaii Pacific Tennis Foundation. Beede then moved to Istanbul, Turkey, to work as director of coaching education and special projects with Gavin Hopper at his international academy of professional players and elite juniors. *Sensei Tennis* is Beede's second book, after publishing *From Go to Pro—a Playing and Coaching Manual for the Aspiring Tennis Player (and Parents): Developing the Elite Tennis Player*. Beede is married and has a grown daughter with two beautiful grandchildren. Now based in Hawaii, Mark loves to travel the world as an observer, tourist, consultant, and promoter for tennis, the sport for a lifetime.

INDEX

A

absolutes. *See* athletic performance: fundamentals of
actions, implicit, 72
alignment rods, 198
anger, 11, 43, 106
angle, 99, 114
  short, 189
  spine, 102, 121, 166
anticipation, xvi, 48, 61–62, 64–65, 68, 72–74, 190, 194
anxiety, 13, 21–23, 26, 32, 43, 115
arc, 54, 124, 165, 172
athletic performance, 46, 107, 199
  components of, xi
  fundamentals of, xi, xiii, 90, 98, 199
attitude, x, xvi–xvii, 11–13, 15–17, 27–28, 47

B

backhand, xi, 24, 123, 142, 145, 152–53, 155, 178, 189
backswing, 39–40
balance, x, xvi, xviii, 7, 28, 43, 60, 64–65, 75–78, 84, 86, 89, 91, 98, 100, 126, 195, 197–98
  athletic, 39, 89
  definition of, 75
  dynamic, 75, 85, 98, 100, 103
  static, 75
balls
  deep, 54, 153, 189–90
  defensive, 110, 191–92
  fast, 39, 63–64, 82–83, 106, 164, 185
  fast deep, 39, 132
  high, 130
  high deep, 129
  high short, 132
  low, 92, 129–31, 143
  macho gorilla, 110
  short, 54, 125, 180, 190, 192
  types of, 132
baseball, xiii, xvii–xviii, 5, 8, 27, 34–35, 40, 61, 63, 67, 76, 85, 90, 98–101, 103–4
basketball, xiii, xviii, 45–46, 75, 86
biomechanics, xiii, xvii–xviii
body alignment, 39, 77, 87
  balanced, 77, 86
  natural law of, 39, 87
Bounce (Syed), 9, 70
boxing, 88, 101, 105
breathing, x, xvi, 41–42

C

calmness, x, xvi, 5, 47
competition, xiii, 14, 28
concentration, xiv, xvi, 16–17, 31, 34–35, 47, 188
  peephole, 31, 34, 36–37, 67
confidence, xvi, 6, 11, 13–14, 16, 26, 47, 199
  lack of, 16, 25
connectedness, xvi, 43, 59, 91, 198
consistency, 35, 117–18
contact point, 65, 69, 79, 92, 125, 137, 142, 193
coordination, 64, 194
core turn, 119, 138, 145
coverage, angle of, 112–13

D

deflection, angle of, 143
discipline, x, 6, 192, 199

213

definition of, 6
distractions, xvi, 16, 31, 36–37
drills
  approach-shot, 185
  approach-volley, 185
  baseline, 193
  chair, 191
  cone, 192
  crosscourt open-court, 184
  cross-step, 190
  defense, 191
  doubles diagonal, 183
  eight-ball, 189
  fastball, 193
  fast serve, 186
  four-ball, 189
  Hopman, 182
  kick serve, 185
  plus-minus, 188
  return-from-the-air, 192
  scrambling, 192
  second-serve-only, 186
  serve and feed, 193
  six-ball, 189
  Spanish, 190
  three-ball forehand, 190
  twenty overhead, 186
  two-ball, 191
  typewriter, 191
  Van Drillen, 187
  X-drill, 190
  yup, 188
Dweck, Carol, 1

E

ego, 12–13, 43, 119, 173, 199
Elderton, Wayne, 65
endurance, xvii, 6, 194, 197
equilibrium, 43, 84–85, 102, 194

F

failure, 4–5, 27
  fear of, 4, 27
fear, 13–15, 22–23, 25–26, 32, 203
flexibility, xvii, 6, 194, 196
fluid motion factor, 70–71
focus, 8, 31–32, 47
  hard, 31, 33–34, 66–67, 69–70, 73, 189, 194
  soft, 31, 33–34, 66–67
focus of attention range (FAR), 65
footwork, 60, 62, 65, 75, 77, 79, 90, 189–90, 195, 197
  keys to, 79
Forbes, Gordon, 22
force, xvi, 38, 96, 106
forehand, 134–35, 137, 142–43, 152, 155, 178, 182, 185–86, 189–90
forehand lag, 137

G

Gallwey, Tim, 17–18, 25, 49, 70, 93
golf, xiii, xviii, 5, 28, 34, 37, 39–40, 85, 88, 93, 100–101, 103, 115
Gould, Dick, x, 202
gravity, center of, 39, 75–76, 85, 88–89, 98–99
grips, 134–35, 151, 163
  bottom-hand Continental to Eastern, 178
  Continental, 135, 155, 163, 178
  Continental to Eastern forehand, 151
  Eastern, 151
  top-hand Eastern to semi-Western, 151, 178
  Western, 134–35

Ground Force, xvi, 39, 77, 80–81, 85, 87–89, 91, 94–96, 125, 127, 174
ground stroke, 24, 39, 55, 92, 111–12, 120–21, 145, 193

H

handshake position, 92, 123, 130, 156, 158, 175–76
hip girdle, 88–89, 97
Hopman, Harry, 182

I

Ickey shuffle, 195
I Feel Your Pain: Let's Make Golf Uncomplicated (Malaska), 5
Inner Game of Tennis, The (Gallwey), 13, 25, 70, 93

J

Jenner, Bruce, 45
jumping rope, 197

K

kata, 6–7
ki, xiv, 38–40, 75, 87, 89
Kiegiel, Ted, 7, 37, 39–40, 43, 76, 85, 87, 97, 103
kinesthetics, 46–47
kinetic chain, xvi, xviii, 40, 43, 74, 77, 87–90, 93–94, 96, 99, 101, 125, 127, 135, 164, 198
kinetic energy, 89, 91, 94, 129
ki one point, 38–39, 89
Koga, Robert, 14–15, 28, 76–77
Koga Method, The (Koga), 14

L

ladder, 194
Laver, Rod, 22

Lee, Bruce, 12, 38
leverage, 77, 80, 91, 93, 100, 135
Loehr, James, 44–45, 48–49
lowest common denominators, xiv, xvi–xvii

M

macho gorilla player, 117
Malaska, Mike, 5, 27–28, 34, 88, 93, 98–100
Maltz, Maxwell, 45
martial arts, xiii, xv, xvii, 28, 38, 40, 43, 60, 66, 75, 87–88, 92, 96, 98, 104–7, 126–27, 199
  basic strategies in, 104
  fundamentals of, xi, xv, 15, 107, 199
  principles of, x–xi, xiii, 92
Martin, Laura, 67, 188
mastery, xv, 6, 30, 70, 72, 74, 203
  personal, xi, 199
  physical, xi, xv
McEnroe, John, 85, 92
medicine ball throw, 195–96
mental toughness, 18
Mental Toughness Training for Sports (Loehr), 44
mind-set
  growth, xvi, 1, 5, 18
  learning, x, xvi, 1, 199
momentum, 97, 100–101
  angular, xvi, 97, 100, 125, 152
  linear, xiv, 97, 100
Murray, John, 44–45, 47–49
mushin, 43–44

N

Nadal, Rafael, 84–85
natural law, xiv, 37, 39, 87, 91, 97–99, 170

net clearance, 112, 127–28, 133, 155
Nichols, Joe, 27
Nicklaus, Jack, 45

O

overheads, 121, 159–60

P

pace, 62, 65, 117–18
perception, xvi, 31, 61–62, 64–65, 67–70, 72–74, 82, 188
performance, xv, 8, 19–20, 28, 32, 39, 43–44, 48, 64, 66, 86, 89
physics, laws of, 96, 98, 101, 174
players
  advanced, 61, 66, 73, 89, 94, 124, 134, 142
  elite, 66
  expert, 65
  intermediate, 66
  right-handed, 123, 153
power zone, 53, 79, 84
practice, purposeful, xvi, 6, 8–9, 182
pressure, 11, 13, 18, 21–26, 114, 182
  adapting to, 26
Psycho-Cybernetics (Maltz), 45
psychosomatics, 49

R

racket-head speed, 93, 120, 125, 128, 136, 151, 163, 186
reaction, xvi, 6, 61, 65, 68–70, 72–74, 188, 194
reaction ball, 70, 74, 194
Reddick, Paul, 67
relaxation, xvi, 36–39, 47, 93, 170
repetitions, 6–7, 25–26, 70, 72, 108, 182
Richardson, Alan, 45

Robson, Tim, xvii–xviii, 4, 8, 27, 34–35, 67, 69, 76, 85, 88, 90, 98–101, 103–4
rotation, x, xvi, 39, 88–89, 96–97, 100
  axis of, 98–99, 101
  sequential, 98–99, 174

S

self-confidence, 14–15, 28
self-control, 14, 28
self-defense, xiii, xvii, 14, 28, 37, 74, 76
setup, xvi, 40, 75, 77, 83, 85–86, 131, 189–90
  balanced, 75, 77, 136
shots
  angled, 114
  approach, 132, 192–93
  defensive, 152
  drop, 55, 155, 161, 191
  macho gorilla, 160
  offensive, 159, 189
  passing, 24, 113, 128, 187
  running, 131
simplicity, xvi, 60, 102
Smart Tennis (Murray), 44
split step, 69, 80–81, 158, 194
stability, 78, 84, 89, 151, 156, 176
steadiness, 7–8
strength, xvii–xviii, 13, 82, 119, 123, 126, 151, 173, 194, 196
Striking Thoughts (Lee), 3, 38
String Theory (Wallace), 8, 71
stroking, 117, 121, 123, 142, 193
Syed, Matthew, 9, 70

T

Tarkenton, Fran, 45
topspin, 102, 123–24, 151, 177
Tyson, Mike, 19

U

unit turn, 119, 135, 151, 178

V

Van Der Meer, Dennis, 161
van Dillen, Erik, 187
visualization, 43–46, 48–49
volleys, xi, 24, 26, 39, 55, 92, 132, 155–56, 158, 162, 178, 182, 185–86, 191, 193

W

Wallace, David Foster, 71
Waske, Alexander, 186
winning, 1–2, 17–18, 32, 115, 203
winning attitude, 15–16
Woods, Ickey, 195
Woods, Tiger, 29

Y

Yellin, Steven, 70–71
yin and yang, xvi, 37–38, 40, 43, 60, 70, 76, 93, 107, 200

Z

Z-ball, 194

Made in United States
Orlando, FL
13 December 2021